SCORE!

MORE
Super Closers, Openers, Reviews and Energizers
for Enhanced Training Results

RICH MEISS and BOB PIKE CSP, CPAE

Creative Training Techniques
Press

S C O R E ! T W O

MORE Super **C**losers, **O**peners, **R**eviews and **E**nergizers
for Enhanced Training Results

by Rich Meiss
and Bob Pike, CSP, CPAE

Design and Layout: Mary Brandenburg
Authors' Illustrations: Cindy Sontag

10 9 8 7 6 5 4 3 2 1

Printed in the United States of America

Publisher
Creative Training Techniques Press
14530 Martin Drive
Eden Prairie, MN 55344
ISBN-13: 978-1-935291-00-8
PRINTED IN THE U.S.A.

For additional books or quantity discounts, contact:
The Bob Pike Group
14530 Martin Drive
Eden Prairie, MN 55344
Phone: 800-383-9210 and 952-829-1954 Fax: 952-829-0260

www.BobPikeGroup.com

C O N T E N T S

SCORE! Two
More
Super
Closers
Openers
Reviews
Energizers
for
Enhanced
Training
Results

SCORE! Two
More
Super
Closers
Openers
Reviews
Energizers
for
Enhanced
Training
Results

ii

THANK YOU

To Mentors, Colleagues and Clients:

As with most things in life, this project would not have been possible without the help and assistance of many people. We thank our many mentors, colleagues and clients with whom we've had the privilege of working throughout our careers in the training and human resource development field. You have sharpened our minds and helped us develop many of the concepts which we now teach.

Thank you to the tens of thousands of presenters, trainers and facilitators with whom we've worked over the last 30+ years. Many of you have given us great ideas, and/or allowed us to try out these ideas in your sessions. We appreciate the chance to work with so many great people, and would also welcome any feedback on the exercises in this book.*

We extend a special thank you to Kenneth Dobrovolny from Aurora, Colorado. A number of the openers and closers included in this book were contributed by Ken and were developed in conjunction with his work at the Colorado Department of Human Services.

Thank you to Mary Brandenburg, Alan Pranke, and Liz Wheeler for their graphic, design and editing skills.

And a special thanks to the loves of our lives, Barbara Meiss and Andrea Pike, for their encouragement to follow through with this project, and then for all their help in seeing it become a reality.

Rich Meiss and Bob Pike

*See "Your Name in Lights" on page 109 for a way to contribute your own activity to another book in this series.

SCORE! Two
More
Super
Closers
Openers
Reviews
Energizers
for
Enhanced
Training
Results

SCORE! Two
More
Super
Closers
Openers
Reviews
Energizers
for
Enhanced
Training
Results

INTRODUCTION

Much so-called training today is a dull combination of lecture and PowerPoint slides. As one trainer remarked, "We are killing them Micro-softly with PowerPoint!" Because most trainers and presenters are given little time to creatively prepare their sessions, they use the easiest and most common form of delivery through lecture, yet we know if participants are exposed to an idea only one time, they will remember less than 10 percent after 24 hours. If we can involve the learners through group discussions and activities, we increase that retention rate to as high as 50 percent. And if we can have participants applying and even teaching the content to each other, **retention soars as high as 90 percent.**

These user-friendly activities and practical exercises are some of the best Bob Pike and I have used in Creative Training Techniques and our other seminars for more than 30 years. They work! Spice up your training with applicable openers and closers. Revisit your content in new and fresh ways. Stimulate and engage your participants with fast energizers. And the great news is you don't have to spend time coming up with these exercises — they are right at your fingertips here in this book!

The book is organized to help you quickly determine an activity or exercise that will work for you and your audience. Choose from these four categories:

Closers — Tie things together and end a session with impact
Openers — Begin a session in a powerful way and draw participants into the content
Reviews — Reinforce key learning in fresh and engaging ways
Energizers — Keep participants mentally stimulated and physically activated

As Bob said in our first *SCORE!* book, this is a cookbook. Rather than reading every page and trying every recipe, use the table of contents to choose what you're hungriest for right now. We know that as you do so, you'll provide a great learning "meal" for your participants — and along the way, you'll greatly enjoy the process.

All good wishes!

Rich Meiss

Rich Meiss
Senior Training Consultant for The Bob Pike Group

SCORE! Two
More
Super
Closers
Openers
Reviews
Energizers
for
Enhanced
Training
Results

SCORE! Two
More
Super
Closers
Openers
Reviews
Energizers
for
Enhanced
Training
Results

HOW TO USE THIS BOOK

Here are four simple steps for using this book effectively:

1. **Remind yourself why it is important** to use closers, openers, reviews and energizers by reading the first page of each chapter.
2. **Select the appropriate category** — closers, openers, reviews or energizers.
3. **Pick the best exercise** based on **PATS MBA** (see the next page).
4. **Practice, practice and practice** the exercise before you actually use it.

Why Use Closers, Openers, Reviews and Energizers?

Each chapter gives more detail about the reasons to use these core exercises in your presentations, but here is a general overview.

Too many presentations simply start and end without a process or purpose. Yet research reveals that people remember best that which they see or hear first and last, so we need to start strong and end strong — using good openers and closers. The purpose of reviews is to make sure the participants really learn the content. A favorite phrase we use is "Just because you said it doesn't mean they learned it." Review multiple times with a variety of methods to ensure learning takes place. And energizers are used to keep participants alive in the session.

What Categories Are Included in the Book?

Although many of these exercises can be used for multiple purposes, we have divided them into four key categories, with Energizers having two subcategories:

Closers

Openers

Review techniques

Energizers

They are the **CORE** to help you **SCORE!** and win in your presentations. Each exercise has been placed into one of these categories and put in that section of the book. In addition, we have often indicated that the exercise may be used for another purpose. For example, several of the review techniques are also good energizers.

How Do I Decide Which Exercise to Use?

There are many details to consider before choosing an exercise. What is my purpose? What do I know about my audience, and will this exercise work for them? What about time and space considerations? What materials do I need, and how much will it cost to purchase them? And will participants be able to gain a learning point and apply it as a result of the exercise?

You can answer these questions briefly by glancing at the format of each page.

SCORE! Two
More
Super
Closers
Openers
Reviews
Energizers
for
Enhanced
Training
Results

Each exercise is explained in detail in the following areas:

Purpose

Audience

Time

Space

Materials

Budget

Application

Also, if applicable, each exercise includes:

Process — the step-by-step procedure for using it

Debriefing ideas or questions

Cautions in using it

Variations with its use

Why Do I Need to Practice the Exercise?

Good presenters make an exercise look easy, but usually that is only because they have used it a number of times. Our experience is that we need to try out an exercise several times — either on some friends and relatives in a low-risk setting, or in front of a mirror by ourselves — before we have the word track and the flow down to use it effectively. Remember the six P's: Proper **P**reparation and **P**ractice **P**revent **P**oor **P**erformance!

Enjoy these **CORE** exercises!

SCORE! Two
More
Super
Closers
Openers
Reviews
Energizers
for
Enhanced
Training
Results

viii

CLOSERS

For many years, we've taught presenters, trainers and facilitators the value of closing their sessions with power. Along with openings, closings are the most valuable real estate that a presenter has, as they form the bookends to the presentation. They should set the stage for the session and **close it off with impact.** Yet too often we hear sessions close with one of these lines:

"Well, our time is up, so we'll see you next time."

"I see our time is up. Please fill out your evaluations. Goodbye!"

These are poor excuses for effective closings! Make sure that you have a closing **ACT**. This includes **A**ction planning, **C**elebration, and **T**ying things together:

A — Action planning, goal setting or reflection time: Give the participants some time to reflect on the important concepts or ideas learned in the session. What are they going to do with the information? How are they going to apply it? By spending some time reflecting and writing, there is a much greater chance they will both retain more of the information and actually apply it. Unfortunately, the opposite is also true. If participants have no time to reflect on the content and think about its application during the program, they will probably not make time to apply their new learning when they return to their jobs.

C — Celebration: Usually participants have invested time, energy — maybe even money — in attending your presentation. They have probably learned new things. Maybe they have gained new skills. They've made difficult decisions, or solved tough problems. They leave having provided useful input. All of these are reasons to celebrate their investment. Celebration can take many forms. It might be something formal, such as certificates of completion given out at a training event, or it might be a more informal celebration — the awarding of small prizes, congratulations from the boss, or even just a quick high-five among the group members for their accomplishment.

T — Tie things together: A great presentation comes full circle and ties the opening and closing together. In a meeting, for example, the agenda is introduced in the beginning and then quickly reviewed at the end. Training sessions circle back to the stated objectives to make sure participants are satisfied with the outcomes. An opening exercise is referred to again as the program is concluded. Then close with a powerful ending — a quote, story, question, or call to action.

Here are some great, proven closers for you to use.

SCORE! Two
More
Super
Closers
Openers
Reviews
Energizers
for
Enhanced
Training
Results

CLOSERS

SCORE! Two
More
Super
Closers
Openers
Reviews
Energizers
for
Enhanced
Training
Results

CLOSERS

CERTIFICATE OF LEARNING

Purpose: This activity allows participants to review key class content while also "celebrating" the learning in the class

Audience: 10 or more

Time: 12 minutes

Space: No extra space needed

Materials: Mock-up of certificates

Budget: Cost of paper

Application: Use this in classes with no formal "learning certificate" as a way to celebrate.

Process: Ask each group to come up with several key learning points they have gained from the class. Their ideas should be the type of statement that could be printed on a completion certificate. Provide a certificate to each participant (see below) that states, "This certifies that _____ has successfully learned _____." Allow 2 minutes for each participant to complete the certificate for himself/herself. Conclude by having them give "high fives" all around!

This certifies that

_____

has

successfully learned

_____.

SCORE! Two More Super Closers Openers Reviews Energizers for Enhanced Training Results

CLOSERS

CLASS QUILT

Purpose: To create a visual reminder of the key learning points from the class

Audience: Best for training audiences of 15–35 seated around tables in small groups of 4–6

Time: 10–15 minutes

Space: Room for participants at flip charts

Materials: Several markers and one sheet of paper per person and one sheet of flip chart paper per group that can be put up with masking tape

Budget: Cost of flip chart paper and markers

Application: In addition to reviewing the class content at the conclusion of a program, this exercise creates a chart that becomes an ongoing review and reminder of the class. The chart can be visually displayed in the work area after the class ends.

Process:

1. Each participant is given one 8½x11-inch sheet of paper along with several different colored markers.

2. Participants are asked to review the class content and then choose one or two key learning points from the session. They then *draw* their key learnings on the sheet. After 5 minutes, they share with their small group their "quilt block" of learning, and each places his block on the chart to form a quilt.

3. Debrief the exercise by having a volunteer in each group share their quilt with the whole group, including their key learning points. To add energy to this exercise, have everyone stand and move to each chart as the chart content is shared.

Cautions: Some participants will be reluctant to draw their learning points. Encourage this as much as possible by modeling a drawing of a learning point yourself. Make sure that your drawing is not too good, even if you draw well, so that those with less drawing talent will be encouraged rather than discouraged.

SCORE! Two
More
Super
Closers
Openers
Reviews
Energizers
for
Enhanced
Training
Results

CLOSERS

COURSE CATALOG

Purpose: To cover course content in a creative way

Audience: 12 or larger

Time: 12–15 minutes

Space: Room for participants at flip charts

Materials: Flip chart and colored markers

Budget: Cost of paper and markers

Application: Use this as a creative review technique or a closing activity.

Process:

1. Using tables as teams, tell each team they have received a request from a local university to add the course they completed today to their course catalog. The university wants to entice their students to enroll in this class.

2. Encourage them to use a maximum of 25 words and create a course description. Tell them to answer this question (you may wish to write this on a flip chart, or have a PowerPoint slide prepared with the question): "What kind of a statement would you write to persuade someone to sign up for the class?" Encourage them to also list the course benefits.

3. Allow 5 minutes to complete this, and ask teams to write their course catalog statement on a flip chart. Report to the larger class when finished. To add energy, have participants all stand and move in front of each of the charts as the statement and course benefits are being read.

SCORE! Two
More
Super
Closers
Openers
Reviews
Energizers
for
Enhanced
Training
Results

CLOSERS

FIRST, NEXT AND LAST

Purpose: To recap key learning points from the session and provide an interactive review or closing activity

Audience: 12 or more divided into small groups of 4–6

Time: 10 minutes

Space: Room for participants at flip charts

Materials: Flip charts and colored markers

Budget: Cost of paper and markers

Application: Allow participants to recap three important elements of the session.

Process:

1. Set one flip chart (or chart paper hung on the walls) around the room for each small group. Have each table group stand by any flip chart in the room.

2. Tell each group they have 1 minute to list the most important "First Thing" that someone should have learned about the class content, and write that on the flip chart.

3. Now tell the groups to rotate clockwise to the next flip chart in the room. Give them 1 minute to now list the "Next Thing" that someone should have learned about today's class. Tell them there should be no repeating of ideas from the prior flip chart or their new chart.

4. Tell the groups to rotate once more, clockwise, to the next available flip chart. Give them 1 more minute to list the "Last Thing" that someone should have learned about today's class. Again, stress that there should be no repeating of ideas from previous flip charts.

5. Have the participants stand and go around the room and get a report from each group of First, Next and Last ideas from each chart. They may then add any new ideas to their individual action plans for the class.

SCORE! Two
More
Super
Closers
Openers
Reviews
Energizers
for
Enhanced
Training
Results

CLOSERS

LEARNING LABB

Purpose: To review key learnings from a seminar or workshop, and make a commitment to take action

Audience: Any size, typically in a training session. This is an individual exercise.

Time: 5 minutes

Space: No extra space required

Materials: One or two LABB sheets per person and pens

Budget: Cost of paper and pens

Application: The main purpose of this exercise is to give participants a chance to write down a goal or action they will take based on ideas they gained from the session. Research proves that people are more likely to act on ideas they have put on paper.

Process:
1. Distribute a LABB sheet, or have participants take a blank piece of paper and write down these four words with some space in between each for writing their thoughts.

   Lesson — What is the most important lesson I learned today?
   Action — What action will I take to get better results?
   Barrier — What barrier(s) will I need to overcome?
   Benefit — What benefit(s) do I expect from taking this action?

2. Give participants 5 minutes or so to write down their thoughts.

3. Have participants share what they wrote down with their learning partner or small group.

Cautions: It is important for people to acknowledge there will be barriers to change — old habits, lack of management support, time constraints, etc. After writing down the barriers, and also listing the benefits of making this change, there is a stronger commitment to actually following through with the new behavior.

Variations: Have several participants share their LABB commitments with the whole group, allowing you to emphasize some key learning points from the program.

CLOSERS

MAGIC COLORING BOOK

Purpose: To amaze your audience while reinforcing an important learning point from the program

Audience: Fewer than 50. Once the audience size grows to more than 50, it is difficult to see the coloring book in the back.

Time: 5 minutes at the most, depending on your story

Space: No extra space required

Materials: One *Magic Coloring Book.* This is an easy-to-use magic prop that adds energy and makes lessons memorable no matter what the training topic. The book is available from The Bob Pike Group at www.BobPikeGroup.com.

Budget: About $20

Application: As with most closers, the application or learning point is emphasized by the story the presenter tells as he or she uses the book.

Process:
1. Decide on a learning point from your topic you'd like to emphasize as you conclude the session. Because we often teach classes on behavioral style/personality, we will use that example here. Ask the audience if it would be okay to close with a little magic.

2. As you hold the book in your hand, begin your story. "Today as we've studied the DISC model, we've learned more about the art and science of dealing with different behavioral styles. Sometimes this information can give us almost magical results in dealing with people.

3. "For example, it seems to me that as we deal with people, it is a little bit like creating a coloring book for our kids or grandkids. We find a book with an intriguing title and colorful cover, but as we open the book, we realize it is just a bunch of blank pages [fan the book with your thumb at the bottom of the pages, revealing only blank pages]. And working with people is sometimes like that as well — we start with a blank page because we don't have a clue as to how to begin."

4. "Well, if we're going to have a coloring book that has value, we all know that we need to have an outline for our kids to color, right?

SCORE! Two
More
Super
Closers
Openers
Reviews
Energizers
for
Enhanced
Training
Results

CLOSERS

MAGIC COLORING BOOK

[Begin to fan the pages at the top, revealing the outlines.] That's what gives kids a framework within which to color. And that is true as we work with people. Their talents, skills and abilities provide a framework for us to better understand them."

5. "But in and of itself, pages with outlines on them are pretty boring, right? Just some black and white frames. What is it that makes a coloring book come alive? (Pause for their answer.) Of course, it is our kids' enthusiasm and participation and coloring ability that transform the dull page into something more beautiful. So let me ask: Are you willing to help me color the book?'"

6. After they say "yes," ask them to think of their favorite color. Then ask them to make a fist and hold that color in their hand. At the count of three, they should "throw" the color at the book. They should also yell the color out loud. Tell them, "If you do this loudly enough and hard enough, you will literally color the book. Ready … one, two, three!"

7. As they throw the color and shout it out loud, pretend to "catch" the colors in the book. Then fan the pages in the center of the book to reveal the colored pages, and say something like this: "Folks, just as it was your enthusiasm, participation and coloring ability that colored our book, so it is our behavioral style that brings color to our everyday human relationships. So take the ideas you have learned today, and apply the magic of DISC to color your relationships and enhance your human interactions. Thanks for being with us today!"

Cautions: Practice, practice, practice. This is a great closer IF you have mastered the motions for the coloring book and IF you have a good story to emphasize one of your key learning points.

Variations: The coloring book process usually stays the same. The variations come in the story you tell as you use it to close your session.

SCORE! Two
More
Super
Closers
Openers
Reviews
Energizers
for
Enhanced
Training
Results

CLOSERS

NEED, SHOULD AND COULD

Purpose: Allow participants the opportunity to reflect on the most important ideas learned from the session

Audience: 12 or more divided into small groups of 4–6 participants

Time: 7 minutes

Space: Room for participants at flip charts

Materials: Flip chart paper, markers

Budget: Cost of paper and markers

Application: Allow members to evaluate the most important aspects of a learning event and think about their application.

Process:
1. Ask participants to join their groups at a flip chart.

2. Ask each group to list these words
   Need
   Should
   Could
   on their flip charts, allowing space to write after each word. Then have them identify two to three ideas participants NEED to know about the subject, one to two things that participants SHOULD be able to do as a result of the training, and one to two resources they COULD tap into to increase their effectiveness on the topic. Have them list their ideas on the flip chart.

3. Have them report their answers to the whole group, thus reinforcing the key learning points and takeaways from the program.

Variations: Another way to position this is to have them write down two to three key NEED TO KNOWs (priority material), several NICE TO KNOWs (addendum material), and one or two WHERE TO GOs (reference material) from the course content.

SCORE! Two
More
Super
Closers
Openers
Reviews
Energizers
for
Enhanced
Training
Results

CLOSERS

10

PASS AROUND

Purpose: Allow participants to reflect on key content learned and rate the best

Audience: Works best in a group of 12 or more

Time: 10 minutes

Space: No extra space required

Materials: 5x7-inch cards

Budget: Cost of cards

Application: This is a fun, interactive way to have students identify what they believe are the most important lessons learned from the class session.

Process:

1. Ask each participant to write one lesson learned from today's class on a 5x7-inch card. Then have everyone stand up (they need a pencil or pen in addition to their card) and walk around and exchange their card with three other people. Now ask them to read this third card and quickly assign a rating to that lesson learned, and write it on the back of the card. (1 = like; 2 = really like; 3 = Super!)

2. Repeat the card exchange with three others, read the new card, assign a rating and write it on the back.

3. Repeat the process one more time for a total of three rounds.

4. Each "Lesson Learned" should now have three different ratings written on the back. Whoever now holds the card should total the three ratings and circle that number.

5. The instructor now asks for anyone holding a card with a rating of "9" to read that lesson learned and the instructor can write it on the flip chart in front. Continue for all ratings of "8" and "7" and "6" until five to eight total lessons learned have been listed.

Variations: As part of your closing, have participants add new ideas from the chart to their goal sheet.

SCORE! Two
More
Super
Closers
Openers
Reviews
Energizers
for
Enhanced
Training
Results

CLOSERS

ROADBLOCKS/ROAD SIGNS

Purpose: To give participants a chance to think about the "roadblocks" to applying their new learning and what they can do to minimize or eliminate these roadblocks

Audience: Any learning group up to about 35 participants divided into smaller groups of 4–6

Time: 12–15 minutes

Space: Room for participants at flip charts

Materials: Flip chart paper, colored markers

Budget: Cost of markers and paper

Application: Every new learning attempt is met with barriers to learning. This exercise gives participants a chance to think of ways to minimize these barriers to learning.

Process:
1. Make flip charts with the following road signs printed at the top:
   Detour   One Way   Merge   Slow Down   Caution   Stop
   Assign each table to one of the signs.

2. Using the chosen topic, ask each table to identify at least five (and up to 10) ways that their road sign might be interpreted or applied to the topic. Give the groups 5 minutes and ask them to write their responses on the flip chart. Report to the entire group when finished.

3. Challenge the groups to minimize or eliminate these "roadblocks" when they get back to their jobs. Brainstorm some "how to do this" ideas if time permits.

Cautions: Be prepared to share an example of a roadblock to get them started.

STRAW THROUGH THE POTATO

Purpose: To help participants do something they didn't think they could do and end with high energy

Audience: More appropriate for training type audiences of 25 or fewer. Be alert for any physical disability with hands or arms that may prevent someone from doing this successfully

Time: 10–15 minutes

Space: Enough room for participants to group around each other and learn how to perform the exercise

Materials: Raw, fairly good-sized baker potatoes (1 per 5 participants), and unwrapped drinking straws (not the flexible kind) — 2 per person

Budget: Cost of potatoes and straws

Application: Multiple learning points can be made from this exercise, including:
- The power of trying something even if you don't believe you can do it
- The importance of follow-through
- The value of teaching someone else how to do something that enhances your own learning

Process:
1. Have several volunteers join you at the front of the room, form a single-file line, and face the audience.

2. Give each participant a clean, raw potato and a regular-sized drinking straw.

3. Ask them, "How many of you believe you can shove this flimsy, plastic straw through this hard, raw potato?"

4. Usually several will be skeptical of their ability to do so. Ask them if they are willing to try, reminding the group that sometimes we just have to try things even if we don't believe we can accomplish them.

5. Explain the process for doing the exercise. Have them hold the potato firmly in their non-dominant hand with a C-clamp grip around the potato. Then have them put the straw in their dominant hand with their four fingers wrapped around the top part of the straw and their thumb firmly in place over the top.

6. Encourage them to practice the striking motion before they actually attempt the exercise. Have them raise their hand to

SCORE! Two
More
Super
Closers
Openers
Reviews
Energizers
for
Enhanced
Training
Results

CLOSERS

STRAW THROUGH THE POTATO

about head level and then quickly plunge the straw downward, continuing the motion until the arm is extended at their side. As they do this, they should repeat the words, "Follow through, follow through" several times. (You can have the audience get involved at this point by having them say the words "follow through" aloud, also.)

7. Tell them when they are ready, they should raise the straw and drive it through the potato, remembering to follow through. If they do not succeed the first time, give them a fresh straw and encourage them to try again. With some patience and encouragement on your part, everyone will be successful.

Cautions: Although we've never had participants really hurt themselves, make sure they are driving the straw through the potato and not their hand, as their striking motion can become quite forceful.

Variations: If there is time and you have enough potatoes and straws, have the volunteers teach other participants in their small group (four to five people) how to do the exercise. In addition to being a great closer, this activity creates tremendous energy in the room. Of course an important key is the story you weave as you teach them to do the exercise. Make sure you close with a powerful story.

SCORE! Two
More
Super
Closers
Openers
Reviews
Energizers
for
Enhanced
Training
Results

CLOSERS

THE "A" GAME

Purpose: To help participants develop a game plan for how they will implement the things they learned in the session

Audience: Any training or learning audience

Time: 5 minutes

Space: No extra space required

Materials: One piece of paper and pencil per participant

Budget: Cost of paper and pencils

Application: Help participants identify their new awareness, things they're going to avoid, and actions they'll take to achieve their learning goals

Process:
1. Have a page in the learner workbook titled *The "A" Game* — or ask participants to take a sheet of paper and label it so. Have them then list the following three **A**'s on the sheet, allowing room underneath each word for them to write comments about the following:

    Awareness Three new ideas they became Aware of during the session
    Avoid   Two things they'll Avoid to get the best results
    Actions   Three Actions they will take to get better results

2. Give participants up to 3 minutes to write down their responses to the three A's, and then have them share their answers with a learning partner or their learning group.

Debrief: Have several participants share with the entire group. Tell the whole group that they will bring their **"A"** game back to their jobs if they will stay Aware of their new learning, Avoid the things that won't work, and take Action on their new ideas!

SCORE! Two
More
Super
Closers
Openers
Reviews
Energizers
for
Enhanced
Training
Results

CLOSERS

TIME FOR "CHANGE"

Purpose: To help participants think about application of the ideas they have learned and how they are going to put them into practice.

Audience: Any size group broken into smaller groups of 4–6

Time: 10 minutes

Space: No extra space required

Materials: 3x5-inch cards; 10 pennies and 2 nickels for each table

Budget: Cost of cards and the amount of change (pennies and nickels) you use

Application: This is a fun way for participants to talk about applying their learning

Process:
1. Put 10 pennies and two nickels on each table. Ask each participant to pick up some change — whatever amount they would like.

2. Tell the students that they will be able to make changes at work tomorrow because of what they learned today — changes that will make them more productive and their jobs easier. Ask them to write on a 3x5-inch card the number of "changes" that they will implement. They should write one idea per the number of cents they picked up. In other words, one penny equals one change, a nickel equals five changes, etc. Give them 2 minutes. Once completed, have the participants share their changes with each other. Go around the room, and ask each group to report several of their changes.

SCORE! Two
More
Super
Closers
Openers
Reviews
Energizers
for
Enhanced
Training
Results

CLOSERS

OPENERS

Most training events and presentations don't have an opener — they just start. The trainer or presenter says something like this:

> "Well, we've got lots to cover today, so let's go!" or
>
> "Our time is short, so let's get started."

Great trainers and presenters recognize that the opening of their event is some of their most precious real estate so they take the time to cultivate a learning atmosphere. They "prepare the soil of the mind" before planting the seeds of learning. To do this, they recognize that they must **"raise the BAR"** with a good opener. A good opener will **Break preoccupation, Allow networking, and Relate to the content.** Here are some additional thoughts on these ideas.

Break preoccupation. Participants come to meetings, presentations and learning events with all kinds of distractions such as how much work they have to do today, what e-mails and voicemails are piling up while they attend this event, what personal or family issues they should be resolving, or what happened that morning on the job. For this reason, a good presenter recognizes that he must break through this preoccupation barrier because it can be the biggest enemy to capturing the full attention of the participants. The key to breaking preoccupation is involvement. Participants can ignore the presenter, but it is difficult to ignore peers when there is a task to accomplish.

Allow networking. Adults usually come to learning events with some experience in the topic. The good presenter will want to tap into that experience throughout the presentation. To accommodate this, the presenter will get the participants acquainted and comfortable with each other. Then throughout the session, she will have them share ideas and experiences with each other thus enhancing the learning for all. Most adults don't want to attend a "sit and get" event; they want to take part, think, contribute and learn. Networking also reduces tension. Participants come into a learning environment wondering: "Can I contribute? Will I fit in? Will anything make me look or feel foolish?" The sooner they get comfortable with each other, the sooner they will become open to learning.

Relate to the topic. Most of your participants want practical take-away value. To demonstrate this value right from the start, the strong presenter will begin with an opener that relates to the content. Poor presenters often start with a story or a joke that might be funny but has nothing to do with the content of the event. Make sure that your opener has a connection to the topic at hand.

Break preoccupation, Allow networking, and Relate to the content. By following these three suggestions, you will find that your opening will raise the **BAR** of your presentation, meeting or training event. Following are some time-tested openers that meet these criteria.

SCORE! Two
More
Super
Closers
Openers
Reviews
Energizers
for
Enhanced
Training
Results

OPENERS

SCORE! Two
More
Super
Closers
Openers
Reviews
Energizers
for
Enhanced
Training
Results

OPENERS

A SWEET OPENER

Purpose: To give participants a chocolate treat while having them relate characteristics of the candy bar to the class content

Audience: Any training or meeting audience

Time: 5 minutes

Space: No extra space required

Materials: Candy bars of mixed types, one for each participant (see suggestions)

Budget: Cost of candy bars

Application: To foster creativity and get the group thinking about the course content

Process:
1. Divide larger groups into teams of four to six, or keep the whole group together if they number fewer than seven.

2. Place one candy bar per person on each table with no duplicates. Have everyone take one.

3. Tell them that before they can eat the candy bar, they have to come up with several ideas to share within their small groups:
   - How is this candy bar like the class content (selling, coaching, teambuilding, etc.)?
   - How is this candy bar like them in the class content (coaching, teambuilding) process?
   - (Come up with your own question to tie the candy to the content.)

4. After several minutes of sharing in small groups, have several people share with the larger group. Then tell them to enjoy their candy while you introduce the topic.
   Examples of candy bars and related characteristics:

Flamboyant	5th Avenue or 100 Grand
Structured	Payday or Zero Bar
Connected	Dots or Smarties
Nutty	Baby Ruth or Nutty Bar
Talkative	Snickers or Whoppers

Variations: Use any type of candy

Cautions: Be alert to any type of peanut allergy

SCORE! Two
More
Super
Closers
Openers
Reviews
Energizers
for
Enhanced
Training
Results

OPENERS

CAN YOU DO IT?

Purpose:	To help participants realize that sometimes it is okay to ask for help
Audience:	Any training or meeting audience
Time:	2 minutes
Space:	No extra space required
Materials:	One 1½-inch rubber band for each participant
Budget:	Cost of rubber bands
Application:	Very often in our jobs and our lives, we believe that we have to "do it myself," as a young child might say. This exercise helps participants recognize that sometimes we CAN'T do it ourselves, and it is okay to ask for help. An application where this has had great success is in any type of abuse training — physical, sexual or emotional — where participants are often reluctant to ask for help. This exercise can help them see that on their own, there is little chance they will be able to solve the problem.
Process:	1. Give each participant a rubber band, and have them hang it from their right thumb.
	2. Ask participants to pull the rubber band along the back of their hand, and then loop it over their little finger, bringing it down as far as it will go on their finger.
	3. Then give them these instructions: "Your goal is to now get the rubber band OFF your little finger so that it is again just hanging from your thumb. However, you may not: Use your other hand; Use your teeth or any other body part, such as your leg; Use a table or any other object. Good luck!" Participants will often struggle with this for some time. After an appropriate time of struggle, say: "I did not say that you couldn't get help from another person." They will then get the hint and have a partner help them remove the rubber band from their finger.
Cautions:	Check the size and tautness of the rubber bands — sometimes they will easily fall off the two fingers or be very easy to work off. You want the exercise to be somewhat difficult.

OPENERS

DIFFERENT EXPECTATIONS

Purpose: Break the ice, provide focus on the topic, and allow opportunities to network

Audience: Minimum of 15; more is better

Time: 15 minutes

Space: Room for participants at flip charts

Materials: Flip charts and markers

Budget: Cost of flip chart paper and markers

Application: To create a fun way for participants to focus on class content and form new groups

Process:
1. Have flip charts pre-labeled. On two charts write "SS" at the top; on two write "AP" at the top. On two more, write "LFO" at the top. Ask the participants to go stand by any one of the six flip charts to form groups of four to six participants.

2. Now, ask each group to list the expectations they have for today's class based on the group they are in. Those who chose the "SS" group are our "Super Stars," so they must list at least six expectations. Those who chose the "AP" group are our "Average Performers," so they must list at least four expectations. Those who chose the "LFO" group are our "Lucky to Find the Office" group so they can only be expected to list one or two expectations.

3. Give the groups 5 minutes to list their expectations before reporting to the entire group.

Cautions: Have some fun, and don't read too much into the groupings. Unfortunately, the reality is that some organizations place different expectations on folks based on prior performance or other assumptions made that are usually incorrect. (You likely will see that the "LFO" group will want to excel, so they may list more expectations than the other groups.)

Variations: Vary the number of charts you put up according to the number of participants in the class. You will want small group sizes of about four to six members each.

SCORE! Two
More
Super
Closers
Openers
Reviews
Energizers
for
Enhanced
Training
Results

OPENERS

FLOCKS OF BIRDS OR PACKS OF ANIMALS

PERSONALITY OPENER

Purpose: To get participants thinking about the course content while breaking them into like "personality" types

Audience: 12 or more

Time: 10–12 minutes

Space: Room for participants at flip charts

Materials: Flip charts and colored markers

Budget: Cost of flip chart paper and markers

Application: Get participants thinking about the characteristics of different personality styles through the use of birds or animals

Process:
1. Have four flip charts pre-labeled with the following:
   Eagle
   Peacock
   Dove
   Owl

2. Ask the participants to choose any one bird and go to that flip chart. After the groups are assembled, ask each group to list at least five or more positive attributes of their chosen bird. Allow 3 minutes.

3. Tell the groups that they will be working with behavioral styles or personality styles today and that each of these birds represents one of the styles. Each style has positive attributes that they've now listed and will be working with throughout the day. Invite them to join their "flocks" at one of the tables in the room.

Variations: Use a "pack of animals" instead of birds. The birds and animals correlate to these behavioral/social styles:

DISC Style	Social Style	Bird	Animal
D – Dominance	Driver	Eagle	Lion
I – Influencing	Expressive	Peacock	Otter
S – Steady	Amiable	Dove	Golden Retriever
C – Cautious	Analytical	Owl	Beaver

OPENERS

GEOGRAPHY QUIZ

Purpose: To help participants recognize that reality is sometimes difficult to discern, so we need to look closely to discover the "real" truth

Audience: Any American audience

Time: 5 minutes

Space: No extra space required

Materials: None

Budget: None

Application: This is a good exercise to have participants examine assumptions while making the point that our "truth" is not always reality.

Process: Tell participants you are going to give them a "Geography Quiz" of three questions in a true-false format. Ask them not to talk to their neighbor or look at anyone else's answers.

Question # 1: Cleveland, Ohio, is northeast of Tallahassee, Fla. – true or false?

Question # 2: Toronto, Ontario, Canada is southeast of Minneapolis, Minn. – true or false?

Question # 3: Los Angeles, Calif., is southeast of Reno, Nev. – true or false?

Give the correct answers — all are TRUE!

Quote speech teacher and former Senator S.I. Hayakawa: "Each of us has in our minds a map of reality. The problem is that the map is not always indicative of the territory."

Ask the group to reflect on this question: What does this little quiz and quote have to do with our topic for today's meeting/training/presentation, which is _____?

SCORE! Two More Super Closers Openers Reviews Energizers for Enhanced Training Results

OPENERS

GETTING TO KNOW ME

Purpose: To provide participants an opportunity to get to know other members of their training class or their small group and build camaraderie and group spirit

Audience: This exercise is most effective in a training audience of 20–30 people

Time: 10 minutes

Space: Enough space for people to get up and move around

Materials: One 3x5-inch card and pen per participant

Budget: Cost of 3x5-inch cards and pens

Application: As participants learn more about one another, they begin to bond at a deeper level and begin to share information more readily. The exercise helps to build trust and fosters an open learning environment.

Process:

1. Distribute a 3x5-inch card to each person in the room.

2. Tell your audience they will have an opportunity to share something unique about themselves by coming up with a quote, song title or saying that best describes them. Once they have determined what that is, have each person write it on the 3x5-inch card.

3. You may want to give some examples that other participants have used:

   "I Did It My Way"
   "Stop and Smell the Roses"
   "You Can Count on Me"
   "When the Going Gets Tough, the Tough Get Going"
   "Duke of Earl"
   "Uptown Girl"

   Once you see that everyone is finished, have them move around the room and share what they wrote with each other. After a few minutes (or when you see that everyone has gotten around the room), have them return to their seats.

Debrief: You can debrief this exercise by asking the following questions: Were there any surprises?

SCORE! Two
More
Super
Closers
Openers
Reviews
Energizers
for
Enhanced
Training
Results

OPENERS

GETTING TO KNOW ME

Were there any similarities?

What does this exercise tell us about our group?

Did you make note of people you wanted to get to know better? (Ha, ha!)

Cautions: If you suspect some negative or inappropriate responses could come up, ask the group to keep this exercise positive or light-hearted.

Variations:

1. If this is a small training class (10 or fewer), you can have participants simply share what they wrote with the entire group.

2. If this is a large training class (50 or more), simply have participants share their responses in their small groups.

SCORE! Two
More
Super
Closers
Openers
Reviews
Energizers
for
Enhanced
Training
Results

OPENERS

HIDE AND SEEK

Purpose: To have participants become better acquainted and to create new table groups

Audience: 12–20 is ideal

Time: 10–15 minutes

Space: No extra space required

Materials: 3x5-inch cards; colored markers

Budget: Cost of cards and markers

Application: This exercise may be useful in sales or service training or any other type of training where it is important *not* to judge people too quickly.

Process: Ask each participant to write one "secret" about himself/herself on a 3x5-inch card (a secret they are willing to share). Collect the cards, shuffle them, and randomly divide them into groups of four cards each. Then read the first four secrets, and ask those four students to stand up without talking. The rest of the class will then guess which secret matches with which student. Repeat the process for each four-person group. This is a good way to divide the class into small work groups immediately before a class exercise. Make points about how we pre-judge people, make snap decisions about them, etc. Point out that it is important to check our first impressions.

Variations: Have five people stand and read their "secrets," and then have them form a group of five.

SCORE! Two
More
Super
Closers
Openers
Reviews
Energizers
for
Enhanced
Training
Results

OPENERS

MAKE A CONNECTION

Purpose: Break the ice, become better acquainted, and allow opportunities to network

Audience: Multiples of 4; minimum of 12

Time: 10–12 minutes

Space: No extra space required

Materials: None

Budget: None

Application: Create teams by having people look at differences and similarities. Use this opener as a way to introduce topics on diversity or behavioral styles.

Process:

1. Ask the participants to form pairs with the stipulation that the person they pick should initially have at least one outward difference from themselves. For example: male/female; different hair color; different color of clothing; relatively "old"/relatively "young," etc.

2. Once paired, ask each pair to now connect by discovering at least three things they have in common. Give them about 4 minutes for this.

3. Now ask each pair to find another pair which has at least one difference. Have them become a foursome and find at least two things they have in common. Give them 5 additional minutes for this. The purpose is to "connect" with others in some way.

4. Then tell them this will be their working group for the class. Have them take 3 minutes and discuss how their "similarities and differences" might relate to the class content. Get group reports, and then transition to class content.

Variations: See "Uniquenesses and Commonalities" on page 34.

SCORE! Two
More
Super
Closers
Openers
Reviews
Energizers
for
Enhanced
Training
Results

OPENERS

MATH MAGIC

Purpose: To drive home the point that practicing certain principles will always yield certain outcomes

Audience: Any training audience

Time: 3 minutes

Space: No extra space required

Materials: Piece of paper and pencil

Budget: Cost of paper and pencils

Application: Certain mathematical principles, when followed, will always yield a specific outcome. Correlate this to other principles that, when followed, will give a certain result. For example, "If you will follow the leadership principles we will teach you today, you too will get a specific outcome!"

Process:
1. Ask participants to take a piece of paper and pencil, and write down a number from 1 to 7. They may choose number 1 or 7 or any number in between.

2. Now multiply that number by 2.

3. Add 5 to that number.

4. Multiply that number by 50.

5. Now, if your birthday date has already come and gone this year, add the number 1758. If your birthday is yet to come this year, add the number 1757.

6. Now think of the year you were born, and subtract that number from your current number (example, 1975). The three-digit number you are left with should equal the following:
   - The first digit is the same one you selected when you started this exercise.
   - The next two digits should be your age.

Cautions: Practice this a few times with friends and family to make sure you are saying the word track correctly. It should work every time!

Variations: In advance of the exercise, turn the flip chart around — or create a PowerPoint slide — and write "4.5 minutes" in big letters on the chart or on the slide.

SCORE! Two
More
Super
Closers
Openers
Reviews
Energizers
for
Enhanced
Training
Results

OPENERS

MATH MAGIC

Tell the group that you are going to take a quick break (or give them a few minutes to do an exercise, etc.), and that it is very important that you agree on the amount of time allowed. Tell the group that you have just written a two-digit number on the flip chart (or you have it posted on your next PowerPoint slide) and that you are going to have them help you predict the number.

Have them take a pen and piece of paper and follow your directions to get to that exact same number. (They should not share their numbers out loud.)

First, they should write down a number *between* 1 and 10 — they may not choose either number 1 or number 10.

Next, have them multiply that number by 9. They should now have a two-digit number, but that number is too big.

Now have them add together the two digits and, since that number is still not quite right, have them divide the number by 2. Say, "That should do it."

Proudly turn your easel around (or expose your next PowerPoint slide) and show them that you also had 4.5. Let them know that is how much time they have for their break (discussion, exercise, etc.)

SCORE! Two
More
Super
Closers
Openers
Reviews
Energizers
for
Enhanced
Training
Results

OPENERS

REACH AS HIGH AS YOU CAN

Purpose: To help participants realize that many barriers are self-imposed

Audience: Any training or meeting audience

Time: 5 minutes

Space: Room at one wall to hang flip chart paper

Materials: Two pieces of flip chart paper, masking tape, and markers

Budget: Cost of flip chart paper, tape and markers

Application: To foster creativity and get the group thinking about possibilities

Process:

1. Tape two sheets of flip chart paper to the wall with one immediately above the other. The bottom of the bottom sheet should be at shoulder height. That will put the top of the top sheet somewhere between nine and 11 feet from the floor (you may need a chair to accomplish this).

2. If your group has 20 participants or fewer, everyone can share the markers and participate. If you have more than 20 participants, divide them into table groups of four to six. Then ask for six to eight volunteers, making sure that each table group is represented by at least one person.

3. Tell the participants to take the cap off the marker, quickly walk by the chart paper, and draw a horizontal line on the chart by reaching as high as they can. Jumping is not allowed.

4. After all the lines are drawn, say: "We know that the average person can actually stretch two to four inches higher than they think they can. So the instructions for the next process are the same: quickly walk by the chart and draw a horizontal line on the chart with the marker by reaching as high as you can. The goal is to reach higher than your previous mark by at least two to four inches."

5. After participants have done this, make an observation about the degree to which each person and the whole group succeeded in reaching higher — even though the instructions were the same. Ask the group for any observations they would make about the exercise. Some answers to look for might include:
   A. Each person did her best the first time, but with some new awareness, she was able to stretch farther the second time.

SCORE! Two
More
Super
Closers
Openers
Reviews
Energizers
for
Enhanced
Training
Results

OPENERS

B. We are often unaware of the artificial barriers we impose on ourselves. By simply focusing on our ability to stretch and grow, we can accomplish even more.

C. The purpose of today's training program (meeting, etc.) is to help us stretch beyond our self-imposed limits and get even better results.

Cautions: Be alert to anyone with physical limitations that would prevent them from participating.

Variations: Tell the group that you believe you can follow the same instructions and place a mark on the paper above all of the others (the shorter you are, the better this works). Take the six markers and snap them together, end to end. Uncap the last marker, and using this new "longer" marker, draw a line near the top of the chart. Make the observation that, by sharing our experiences and resources with one another, we can all help each other reach higher than we think we can.

SCORE! Two
More
Super
Closers
Openers
Reviews
Energizers
for
Enhanced
Training
Results

OPENERS

THE 2ND, 3RD AND 4TH RIGHT ANSWERS

Purpose: To help participants understand that sometimes there are several "right" answers to a question or problem — some things don't have to be done just one way

Audience: Any training or meeting audience

Time: 3 minutes

Space: No extra space required

Materials: Flip chart pad or PowerPoint slide

Budget: Cost of flip chart paper

Application: When training certain types of content, it is important to recognize that there are several "right" answers. For example, in managing people, there might be several effective ways to redirect behavior. By doing this exercise in a session, you help participants understand that there could be several ways to complete this management task.

Process:
1. Write the following equation on a chart, or put it on a PowerPoint slide:

   ½ of 8 = _____.

2. Most participants will write 4, look at you smugly, and put their pens down.

3. Ask what the answer is. After someone says 4, ask if there are any other answers.

4. Additional "right" answers include: 2 squared; eic, jht (the word "eight" spelled out, then cut in half in the middle of the g); 3, E (the number 8 cut down the middle); 0 (two zeros on top of each other form an 8), etc.

Cautions: You'll probably get a few groans on this one.

THINKING SYSTEMATICALLY

Purpose: To help participants think in terms of systems, not just parts

Audience: Any training or meeting audience

Time: 3–5 minutes

Space: No extra space required

Materials: A printout, slide or chart of these two puzzles

Budget: Cost of paper

Application: Sometimes we have to think of the whole system rather than just the parts. This is a great exercise when you want participants to see the whole of something.

Process: Hand out a sheet (or write on a flip chart or project on a PowerPoint slide) with the following two puzzles:

Punctuate the following:

that that is is that that is not is not is that it it is

Answer: That that is, is. That that is not, is not. Is that it? It is.

Decipher the following (determine what the sentence says) by substituting different letters for the ones written here:

M Z Q P Q L P Q A Z Q X U C M X C T F Q X A Q P F Q L P ?

Hint: After they struggle with this puzzle, ask them to notice the punctuation at the end. If this is indeed a question, ask them to think of what word might start the question. Once they figure out the first word (Where), they can then use the letter substitutes (M=w, Z=h, Q=e, P=r, etc.) to figure out the rest of the sentence.

Answer: Where are the snows of yesteryear?

SCORE! Two
More
Super
Closers
Openers
Reviews
Energizers
for
Enhanced
Training
Results

OPENERS

UNIQUENESSES AND COMMONALITIES

Purpose: To help participants get acquainted in an interesting way and to connect the insights learned to the topic of the day

Audience: Any size subdivided into small groups of 4–6

Time: 5–10 minutes

Space: No extra space required

Materials: Paper and pens

Budget: Cost of paper and pens

Application: As human beings, we each have some unique things about us, but we also have much in common. Today's session will help us explore some of these uniquenesses and commonalities (great for diversity training or personality training, such as that using DISC, Social Styles, or Myers-Briggs models).

Process:

1. Ask each member of the group to draw a fairly large circle in the center of a piece of paper, leaving some room both inside and outside the circle to print some information.

2. On the outside of the circle, have them write the names of each of their group members and draw a blank line below each name.

3. On the inside of the circle, have them write the numbers 1, 2 and 3.

4. Tell the participants that they will have 5 minutes to complete the exercise. Through a process of discussion, they are to find and write down one thing about each small group member that is unique to him or her (not true of anyone else in the group) and three things they all have in common in their group.

5. Tell them to avoid things that are obvious or assumable. For example, someone might say, "I am the only male at this table," which is probably obvious. Have them try to discover unique and interesting things such as "I am the only group member who was born in another country."

6. When they look for the three commonalities, have them avoid things like "We are all here at the seminar together" (too obvious), but have them find things such as "We are all chocoholics!"

SCORE! Two
More
Super
Closers
Openers
Reviews
Energizers
for
Enhanced
Training
Results

OPENERS

UNIQUENESSES AND COMMONALITIES

7. Remind them they are looking for one unique thing about each group member and three things they have in common. Remind them they have 5 minutes, answer any questions they may have and instruct them to begin.

8. At the conclusion of the exercise, you may do one of two things, or both. If you have the time, people usually enjoy hearing the uniquenesses and commonalities of each group. Minimally, have them tell you what some of the learning points are from the exercise, and make sure to show them how this connects to your topic.

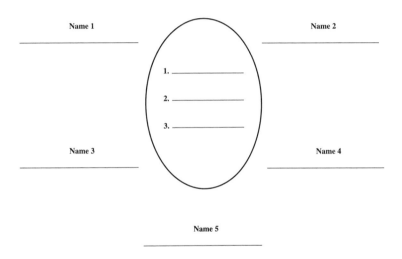

Name 1

Name 2

1. _____

2. _____

3. _____

Name 3

Name 4

Name 5

Cautions: Keep encouraging participants to finish, as sometimes they will have difficulty completing the task in 5 minutes.

Variations: See "Make a Connection" on page 27.

SCORE! Two
More
Super
Closers
Openers
Reviews
Energizers
for
Enhanced
Training
Results

OPENERS

WHAT, WHY AND HOW

Purpose: To allow the trainer an opportunity to learn about participant needs in the class while also pairing participants up with a learning partner

Audience: 12 or more

Time: 10 minutes

Space: No extra space required

Materials: One 3x5-inch card for each participant

Budget: Cost of cards

Application: This activity creates "buy-in" for the participants from the beginning of the class and also gives the instructor valuable information about the participants

Process:

1. After introducing the class content and objectives, have each participant take a 3x5-inch card and write these three words down the left-hand side:
   What
   Why
   How

2. Have each participant then write down an answer on the card to these three questions:
   "What" is the most important thing you'd like to learn today?
   "Why" do you believe that will be important to learn?
   "How" do you best like to learn? Do you learn best through lecture, hands-on activities, a lot of visuals, case studies, etc.?

3. Ask the participants to pair up with someone sitting at a different table and share their whats, whys and hows.

4. Then tell the pairs to find another pair and form a table group. As a group, they should come up with their two most important whats, whys and hows.

5. Allow the groups 3 minutes to discuss and agree, and then ask all groups to report out to the entire group.

SCORE! Two
More
Super
Closers
Openers
Reviews
Energizers
for
Enhanced
Training
Results

OPENERS

WHAT'S THE ORDER?

Purpose: To cause participants to "think outside the box"

Audience: Any training or meeting audience

Time: 5 minutes

Space: No extra space required

Materials: Slide, whiteboard or flip chart

Budget: None

Application: Our tendency as human beings is to get caught in the limitations of our own thinking. This exercise is very difficult for most participants to figure out as the mind sees "letters" and has a hard time translating that to "numbers" and vice versa. Use the exercise(s) to stimulate some new ways of thinking.

Process: Put the following numbers on a slide, and ask participants to fill in the last three blanks. After a minute or so (if no one has come up with the answer), give them this hint: "Think numbers and not letters."

O T T F F S S __ __ __

Solution: The "letters" are actually the first letter of the numbers; i.e. O = 1, T = 2, T = 3, F = 4, F = 5, S = 6, S = 7. The correct answers for the final three blanks would therefore be E (for Eight), N (for Nine), and T (for Ten).

After someone has guessed the correct answer or you have revealed it, ask the group to discuss how this exercise might be like the topic of today's meeting or lesson.

Variations: List the following letters and ask participants to complete the last three blanks. (This time, your hint for them would be to think letters and not numbers.)

8 5 4 9 1 7 6 __ __ __

Solution: The numbers, spelled out and alphabetized, would fall into this arrangement: Eight, Five, Four, Nine, One, Seven, Six – so the fill-in numbers would be 3, 2, 0 (Three, Two, Zero spelled out and alphabetized).

SCORE! Two More Super Closers Openers Reviews Energizers for Enhanced Training Results

OPENERS

WORLD'S EASIEST QUIZ

Purpose: To show that what something is called is not always what it really is

Audience: Any training or meeting audience

Time: 3–5 minutes

Space: No extra space required

Materials: None

Budget: None

Application: To show that what is in a name or a title isn't necessarily an accurate depiction of the subject

Process: Copy the quiz printed on the next page and have participants answer the questions, or read the questions and have participants volunteer their answers.

Cautions: Be careful not to make participants feel stupid with this quiz. The main purpose is to show that what something is called is not always an accurate depiction of what it is.

Quiz Answers:
1. 116 years
2. Ecuador
3. Sheep or horses
4. November
5. Squirrel fur
6. Dogs
7. Albert
8. Crimson
9. New Zealand
10. Orange

SCORE! Two
More
Super
Closers
Openers
Reviews
Energizers
for
Enhanced
Training
Results

OPENERS

WORLD'S EASIEST QUIZ

Write your answers to this "easy" quiz. Four out of ten will be a passing grade.

Questions:

1. How long did the Hundred Years War last?   _____

2. Which country makes Panama hats?   _____

3. From which animal do we get catgut?   _____

4. In which month do Russians celebrate the October Revolution?   _____

5. What is a camel's hair brush made of?   _____

6. The Canary Islands in the Pacific are named after what animal?   _____

7. What was King George VI's first name?   _____

8. What color is a purple finch?   _____

9. Where are Chinese gooseberries from?   _____

10. What is the color of the black box in a commercial airplane?   _____

SCORE! Two
More
Super
Closers
Openers
Reviews
Energizers
for
Enhanced
Training
Results

OPENERS

OPENERS

REVIEWS

UCLA communications professor Albert Mehrabian did a research study to determine how often a person needs to be exposed to ideas in order to remember the majority of them. His research determined the following:

Exposed to an idea one time: after 30 days, retention is less than 10 percent

Exposed to an idea six times: after 30 days, retention is greater than 90 percent (especially if there is "interval reinforcement," such as revisiting the idea after an hour, after a day, after three days, after a week, etc.)

Mehrabian's research suggests that to help people learn, **we need to cover a concept or idea at least six times,** allowing some time lapse in-between the reviews. Yet, most learning events today cover ideas one time and expect the participants to remember them. Maybe the reason this happens is that trainers believe that it is boring to repeat themselves over and over. But doing a revisit doesn't have to be boring. Creative trainers and presenters find interesting ways to **allow the participants to do the revisit,** which makes it more interesting and effective. So here's the key: review is when the trainer does it, and revisit is when the participants do it. Therein lies the power — getting the participants to revisit.

Here are some tips for helping participants learn more in your sessions:

Revisit early and often. Remember, we need to cover key content at least six times for maximum retention.

Don't call it "review." In our sessions, we suggest that trainers avoid the "R" word — "review" — and instead use the word "revisit." The difference is that the instructor is the one who usually does a review, covering the content again, while in a revisit the participants are going over the content another time in a more interesting way.

Use a variety of revisit techniques. This keeps the interest level of participants high and helps them stay engaged in the learning process.

The following pages contain some of our favorite review and revisit techniques. Each is very powerful. Enjoy learning and employing these techniques, knowing that ultimately your learners will be the ones to benefit!

SCORE! Two
More
Super
Closers
Openers
Reviews
Energizers
for
Enhanced
Training
Results

REVIEWS

REVIEWS

A BIT FROM THE BOOK

Purpose: To provide participants the opportunity to reinforce key concepts by reading and sharing from a reference book on the topic

Audience: Any size group divided into table groups of 4–6

Time: 20–30 minutes

Space: No extra space required

Materials: One reference book per participant

Budget: Cost of reference books

Application: Use as a revisit activity, or use as a way to teach additional content on the topic

Process:
1. Assign each participant in a small group a chapter or section of the reference book. Give participants a certain time period (usually 10 to 15 minutes) to scan through his assigned section, highlighting or noting the key points from that section.

2. After the study time is up, give each participant 2 to 3 minutes to share three to five points he learned from his assigned section. Encourage the other group participants to follow along, marking the pages or highlighting the information in that section that is valuable to them. Continue the process around the group, until all have shared.

3. If appropriate, have a Q&A session on the content covered, or give participants a few moments to reflect on what they learned and add any key ideas to an action idea list.

Cautions: Although this takes some time, it is a great way to familiarize participants with valuable resource information.

Variations: Encourage participants to teach the information in a creative way. They may do a skit, create a visual presentation of the information, or find some other creative way to present it. Note: this variation will probably take more time, but it is more fun and engaging.

SCORE! Two
More
Super
Closers
Openers
Reviews
Energizers
for
Enhanced
Training
Results

REVIEWS

A HELPING HAND

Purpose:	To provide participants the opportunity to reflect on the key learning points of the class in an unusual way
Audience:	Any size group divided into table groups of 4–6
Time:	5 minutes
Space:	No extra space required
Materials:	Hand-shaped sticky notes
Budget:	Cost of sticky notes
Application:	Use as a review activity or a closer

Process:

1. Ask each student to write one or two ideas on the hand-shaped sticky notes. The action ideas should be tips on how to best use some class content.

2. Once completed, have a table volunteer collect all the sticky notes from his table, and post them on a piece of flip chart paper in front. Read all of the ideas aloud to the class. A great follow-up by the instructor would be to compile all the ideas in a summary format and send them to all class participants.

Cautions: Use regular sticky notes if you cannot find the hand notes.

Variations: Ask participants to form groups of three to four people based on identical or similar hand size. Check palm to palm for size. Once the groups are formed, ask each group to trace one hand on a flip chart page and then identify and list five (one for each finger and thumb of the hand) objectives they want to learn from today's class (as an opener) or lessons they have learned from the session (as a closer). Give them 5 minutes to list, and then report out.

The best list can be voted on by the rest of the class with applause (giving them a hand). Award prizes if appropriate.

SCORE! Two
More
Super
Closers
Openers
Reviews
Energizers
for
Enhanced
Training
Results

REVIEWS

ALPHABET SEARCH

Purpose: To help participants revisit the content of the class

Audience: From 10 to 50 participants. Smaller training audiences can do this at wall charts in groups of 4–6; larger groups would need to do it at their tables

Time: 5–7 minutes

Space: No extra space required

Materials: Flip chart paper, tape and markers, or blank sheets of paper

Budget: Cost of paper, tape and markers

Application: This exercise is a celebratory and interactive way for participants to review key content covered in the training session.

Process:
1. Have each team get a piece of flip chart paper, some masking tape and a set of markers, and then have them hang their flip chart paper on the wall.

2. Have them draw a line down the middle of the chart and write the letters A–M down the left side of the chart and the letters N–Z down the middle of the chart.

3. Have the teams gather around their charts. When you give the signal, have them begin writing down words, ideas or concepts that have been covered in class that begin with each of the letters of the alphabet. Make sure they are all engaged in the writing.

4. Call time after 5 minutes. You may debrief by having someone from each team call out the words they came up with for each letter.

5. Be flexible with the more difficult letters. For example, "X" could be something "x-tra."

Cautions: Make sure everyone participates and no one person dominates the activity.

Variations: Have this become a competition with the winning team being the one to complete the most letters in 5 minutes.

SCORE! Two
More
Super
Closers
Openers
Reviews
Energizers
for
Enhanced
Training
Results

REVIEWS

BOOK, MOVIE OR SONG

Purpose: This is a creative, interactive way to revisit content

Audience: Any learning audience of about 10–30 participants

Time: 15 minutes

Space: Room for participants at flip charts

Materials: Flip chart paper; colored markers

Budget: Cost of markers and flip chart paper

Application: Longer class sessions may need some active reviews to keep people learning and to make the learning more fun and interactive. This will work especially well in energetic, extroverted groups.

Process:

1. Ask each participant to choose a favorite pastime: reading a book, watching a movie, or singing a song. Have them break into small groups of four to six according to these pastimes. (You may have several groups of book readers, etc., if the whole group is over 15 people.)

2. Ask each group to choose one or two titles (book, movie or song title) which best describe the content of today's class and discuss why they chose that title. Tell them that the readers are then going to give a short book report on class content, the movie-goers are going to act out class content, and the singers are going to sing aloud class content — based on the book, movie or song they chose.

3. Allow about 10 minutes for preparation, and then have all groups perform for the larger class.

Cautions: Some will be reluctant to sing or act. If so, they may choose to also give a book report.

Variations: Have all the groups just give a book report on their titles and how they relate to the class content.

SCORE! Two
More
Super
Closers
Openers
Reviews
Energizers
for
Enhanced
Training
Results

REVIEWS

DICEY REVISIT

Purpose: To give participants a fun and interactive way to revisit content while also creating an energizing environment

Audience: Any training or learning audience seated in small groups at tables

Time: 5 minutes

Space: Space at tables to roll a die

Materials: One large die at each table

Budget: Cost of dice

Application: Use the concept of revisiting key content at least 6 times to drive home the main learning points of a training session.

Process:

1. Purchase enough large dice so that you have one for each small group in a training session (available online at www.BobPikeGroup.com).

2. Prepare the dice by putting sticky notes on each side, and then write a concept, term or learning point from the program on each sticky. Each sticky on every die should be different. With traditional dice, you would need 24 different ideas for four dice. Tape the sticky notes on so they do not fall off during the dice toss.

3. After covering certain key content, place one die on each table. Have the members of that table group take turns rolling the die and defining the key term or listing the main learning points of the content heading they rolled. Continue the process until all six sides of the die have been covered (about 3 minutes).

4. Call time, and then continue the teaching process. At appropriate times, call for a "dicey revisit," have table groups rotate the dice to other tables, and repeat the process.

SCORE! Two More Super Closers Openers Reviews Energizers for Enhanced Training Results

REVIEWS

DUELING FLIP CHARTS

Purpose: To create an interactive review process that creates some light competition

Audience: Any training audience of 20 or fewer

Time: 5–10 minutes

Space: No extra space required

Materials: Two easels with flip chart paper and several markers

Budget: Cost of flip chart paper and markers

Application: Use this technique in a class that has a lot of learning points. This method allows for a quick review of ideas.

Process:

1. Ask for two volunteers from the class who are comfortable writing on a flip chart. Ask the volunteers to choose a favorite color marker and approach one of the two flip charts in the front of the room.

2. Have the volunteers label their charts with the words "Key Ideas." They are to then capture on their chart key ideas mentioned by participants, alternating back and forth as the process unfolds.

3. Ask the balance of the participants to stand by their chairs. Tell them you are going to go around the class, asking each participant in succession to share one key learning point from the session. As they share their point, it is written down on one of the charts. Continue around the group until everyone has shared.

4. Go around the group again, telling participants that they may say "pass" and have a seat when they no longer have any ideas. Continue until no ideas are left.

Cautions: Encourage participants to avoid duplication of ideas if possible

Variations:

1. Turn this into a competition to see who can be the "last one standing." Award a prize.

2. Put a vertical line down each flip chart. Get two scribes per flip chart — preferably two left-handed and two right-handed people. Have one "leftie" and one "rightie" at each flip chart. Do the scribing as above, but you can accelerate the capture time with more scribes.

FLIP CHART LEARNING POINTS

Purpose: Allow small groups the opportunity to work as pairs and provide a recap of course content

Audience: Any size training audience broken into pairs

Time: 12–15 minutes

Space: Room for participants to walk to and between flip charts

Materials: Flip chart paper and markers

Budget: Cost of flip chart paper and markers

Application: To allow a creative revisit of the learning content

Process:
1. When it is time to review and energize, post six blank flip chart sheets on various walls of the training room.

2. List a "content chunk" at the top of each chart. In a train-the-trainer program, the six topics might be: Opening, Closing, Revisiting, Energizing, Learner Motivation, and Dealing with Difficult Participants.

3. Challenge each pair to visit each flip chart two or three times to list or draw a learning point about the training content. No point can be repeated on a flip chart, and only one point can be listed at a time.

4. When you say "go," the pairs should race around the room to write or draw simple pictures of each point. When the time is up, each pair will have listed from 12 to 18 significant points from the class.

5. Then divide the class into small groups of three to seven people, and have them visit each chart, adding ideas to their individual action plans. They should also circle any item they do not understand. At the end of the exercise, all circled items can be explained by the contributors of that idea.

SCORE! Two
More
Super
Closers
Openers
Reviews
Energizers
for
Enhanced
Training
Results

REVIEWS

HUMAN FLOW CHARTS

Purpose: To create an interactive way to review content sequences

Audience: Any training audience

Time: 5–10 minutes

Space: Enough space for participants to demonstrate the process or steps visually

Materials: 3x5-inch cards

Budget: Cost of cards

Application: Use this process as an interactive review for content sequences. If you are teaching the nine steps of The Hug of Life (also known as the Heimlich Maneuver, which can dislodge a foreign object from someone's throat), give participants a 3x5-inch card with one step on it as you teach the step. The card could have a drawing on it or the step written out.

Process:

1. Make up 3x5-inch cards with the various steps of a sequence, either listed by name or shown in some pictorial form.

2. As you teach the concept, hand the card with that concept to one participant, telling her to be alert for an opportunity to use the card later.

3. After teaching all the steps, say, "Let's create a human flow chart." Participants are to get up from their chairs, go to an open space in the room, and put themselves in the proper position to model the successful execution of the process. For example, in the case of the nine steps of The Hug of Life, they would line up single file in the correct order to perform the procedure.

4. Once the correct order or flow is achieved, have each person explain (or demonstrate) their step or concept.

Variations: Rotate the cards among participants to give all a chance to revisit.

KEY CONCEPTS "TEACH BACK"

Purpose: To allow participants to summarize the key concepts of the program

Audience: Training audience of any size broken into groups of 4–6

Time: 10–15 minutes

Space: Room for participants at flip charts

Materials: Flip charts and colored markers

Budget: Cost of flip chart paper and markers

Application: By having participants teach each other, they are reinforcing the key concepts of the program. Therefore, they'll be more likely to remember them.

Process:
1. Tell the participants they should assume that they will be delivering training on today's topic to others who could not attend. Have the groups gather around their flip charts.

2. Tell each group that they only have one piece of flip chart paper to use. They are to identify the most important concepts of the program and may display that concept any way they choose. They may use words, diagrams, pictures, cartoons or anything else they wish.

3. Allow 5 minutes for them to complete their task. Then have the entire group visit each chart, allowing each group to "teach" the main ideas of the program in 2 minutes.

SCORE! Two
More
Super
Closers
Openers
Reviews
Energizers
for
Enhanced
Training
Results

REVIEWS

PRIORITY DOTS

Purpose: Allow time for the development of action ideas both individually and as a large group

Audience: Any size training audience

Time: 12–15 minutes

Space: No extra space required

Materials: One or two sheets of flip chart paper, markers, sticker dots of varying colors

Budget: Cost of flip chart paper, markers and a box of ¾-inch Post-it brand dots of various colors

Application: To create a prioritized action idea list

Process:

1. Have your participants create an action idea list from the beginning of your presentation. At some point, have them capture all the ideas on flip charts. The result will be several flip charts that contain a complete list of the action ideas.

2. At the halfway point of the session, distribute five different colored dots to each participant.

3. Have the group decide which color will represent first, second, third, fourth, and fifth choices (i.e., red color = 1st choice, green = 2nd choice, etc.).

4. Each participant then votes for their top five action ideas by placing one of their colored dots next to it.

5. Near the end of the session, repeat the process by creating action idea charts for the second half of the session. Participants then remove their original votes and vote for the top five ideas for the entire session — in priority order.

Variations: Have participants vote for the top five without prioritizing.

SCORE! Two
More
Super
Closers
Openers
Reviews
Energizers
for
Enhanced
Training
Results

REVIEWS

PUZZLE POWER

Purpose: To use a variety of puzzles to review (or preview) key content

Audience: Any training or learning audience

Time: 5–10 minutes

Space: No extra space required

Materials: Usually one piece of paper per participant

Budget: Cost of paper and printing

Application: These puzzles can be used as openers, closers, energizers or reviews of content

Process:
1. Go to www.puzzlemaker.com on the Web. Puzzlemaker is a puzzle generator for teachers. Select the appropriate puzzle you wish to use. Puzzles currently available (as of the publication date of this book) are:

Criss-Cross	Cryptograms	Double Puzzles
Fallen Phrases	Hidden Messages	Letter Tiles
Math Squares	Mazes	Number Blocks
Word Search		

2. Choose the puzzle you wish to use. Then add your own content, hit the enter button, and "voila!" you have your puzzle.

3. Use the puzzle as a review of your key content.

Variations: Use the puzzles as openers, closers or energizers as well as a review. A common use of either Crossword Puzzles or Word Search is to build in some of your jargon, acronyms and abbreviations, and have participants complete the puzzle at the beginning of class. You may then explain how these terms will be used and clarified in the program.

SCORE! Two
More
Super
Closers
Openers
Reviews
Energizers
for
Enhanced
Training
Results

REVIEWS

QUESTION BEE

Purpose: To use the concept of a "Spelling Bee" as a way to review content

Audience: Any training or learning audience of 20 or fewer

Time: 10 minutes

Space: Enough for 2 groups to line up on opposite sides of the room

Materials: Prizes (candy suggested)

Budget: Cost of candy

Application: Create friendly competition to review the key concepts

Process:

1. In advance of the program, create a series of questions that will review the content of the program. They can be any type of questions — true/false, matching, fill-in-the-blank, or essay questions. Create questions of low, medium and high difficulty.

2. Divide the class into two teams, and have each team form a single-file line on opposite sides of the room. Tell them that you are going to have a "question bee" similar to the old-fashioned "spelling bee" some of them may remember from school days. Each team will get a point each time one of their team members correctly answers a question.

3. Begin with the first person on the first team, and ask one of your questions. If that person answers correctly, his team gets a point. If he answers incorrectly, the first person on the opposite team gets a chance to answer the question. Continue asking questions and assigning points until you have run out of questions or everyone has had a chance to answer a question. Try to even out the level of difficulty of questions for both teams.

4. Determine the winning team, and give out a small prize.

Cautions: Caution participants not to shout out answers until it is their turn.

Variations:

1. Pass or Play. As above, but the person being asked the question can either choose to answer or can pass it to the next person on the other team. Double points are awarded if the challenged person can answer it for their team.

2. We "get by with a little help from our friends." As above, but half the point value if anyone on the team can answer before it passes to the opposing team.

SCORE! Two More Super Closers Openers Reviews Energizers for Enhanced Training Results

REVIEWS

QUIZ CARDS

Purpose: To create a double revisit of content by having participants write the questions that will be used on the quiz

Audience: Any training audience

Time: 5–10 minutes

Space: No extra space required

Materials: 3x5-inch cards

Budget: Cost of cards

Application: Use this technique when you want to cover content multiple times for maximum learning and retention

Process:
1. On the second or third day of a multiple-day training program, give each participant a 3x5-inch card. On the card, have them write a question from content already covered that other participants should be able to answer. The question may be in any form — true/false, fill-in-the-blank, matching, or essay.

2. Collect the cards, and read through them to eliminate duplicates and refine them.

3. Tell the group they are going to do a question and answer quiz. You may carry it out in one of these ways:
   - You, the instructor, read the questions and ask the group to answer them, either in writing or verbally; or
   - Shuffle the cards and divide them equally among the small groups. Have the participants answer them in their groups. Rotate the cards to other groups and, after several rounds, clarify any questions or answers that are unclear.

Cautions: Allow participants to use their "open books" for writing their quiz questions if you believe they will not be able to write good quiz questions otherwise.

SCORE! Two More Super Closers Openers Reviews Energizers for Enhanced Training Results

REVIEWS

TEACHING THROUGH TRIVIA

Purpose: To create a fun and interactive revisit technique by creating trivia questions around your course content

Audience: Any training or learning audience you can divide into teams

Time: 5–10 minutes

Space: No extra space required

Materials: Prizes

Budget: Cost of prizes

Application: Take advantage of the popularity of trivia games and questions to review content in a fun way.

Process:

1. Write up a set of trivia questions that cover different aspects of your course content. You might have different categories of questions. In a sales program, you might have categories around prospecting, interviewing, demonstrating and closing.

2. After teaching content, divide the group into teams and play a form of trivial pursuit. To avoid any controversy about the answer they wish to use, each team must say "Our final answer is ..." before giving their answer. When they use this phrase, they are no longer permitted to change their answer.

3. To create a competitive atmosphere, give points and award prizes at the end.

Variations: To save you time in coming up with questions (and also to create a double revisit), have the participants come up with questions from the course content. The best way to do this is to give out 3x5-inch cards, then have them write one question on one side of the card with the answer to that question on the opposite side. You can then collect the cards and choose the questions you wish to use in the trivia game.

SCORE! Two
More
Super
Closers
Openers
Reviews
Energizers
for
Enhanced
Training
Results

REVIEWS

30-SECOND ADVERTISEMENT

Purpose: Allow small groups the opportunity to work as a team and provide a recap of the course content

Audience: Any size training audience broken into small groups of 4–6

Time: 12–15 minutes

Space: No extra space required

Materials: Piece of paper and pens

Budget: Cost of paper and pens

Application: To prepare a creative revisit of the learning content

Process:
1. Have the participants work at their table teams for this exercise. Tell them their assignment is to prepare a 30-second advertisement for today's class.

2. Have them identify one to three quick "selling points" that would appeal to another audience and entice them to enroll in the class. Their task is to write this out in the form of an advertisement on a sheet of paper, and be prepared to share it with the whole group.

3. Allow 6 minutes to prepare, and then have one group member read their advertisement to the entire group. Continue until all groups have shared. You may award a prize to the most creative group if you desire.

Variations: Teams could perform their advertisement in the form of a song or skit.

SCORE! Two
More
Super
Closers
Openers
Reviews
Energizers
for
Enhanced
Training
Results

REVIEWS

WALL TALK

Purpose: To allow the development of action ideas individually

Audience: Any size training audience

Time: 12–15 minutes

Space: No extra space required

Materials: None

Budget: None

Application: To allow for reflection time

Process:
1. Ask each person to stand, walk to the nearest wall and form groups of three people, each containing not more than one person from their current table.

2. Each small group discusses, "What is the most useful thing you've learned so far?" After 3 minutes, have people move into new groups of five, none of whom were in the group of three.

3. Each person shares an important lesson learned that they just received from someone in their group of three.

4. Participants return to their original tables and share their single most important lesson learned from all they've heard, including their original lesson learned.

Variations: Have the last group of five become a new group that forms at a new table. Participants gather their materials and meet at a new table.

SCORE! Two
More
Super
Closers
Openers
Reviews
Energizers
for
Enhanced
Training
Results

REVIEWS

ENERGIZERS

Mental Stimulators create a "mental spark" that also energizes the body.

Great presentations and training sessions keep participants energized through the use of effective presentation methods as well as mental stimulators and physical energizers. This section of *SCORE! Two* offers a variety of energizers to **keep participants active and engaged.**

Energizers are useful throughout a session and probably are most useful during these times: after lunch, after a break, when the room temperature is too warm, and during the middle of a long content presentation.

This section contains two types of energizers. Part one of this section is Mental Stimulators. These activities create mental sparks that stimulate the brain and **keep participants ready to learn.** This set of activities includes memory stimulators, trivia tests, quizzes and thought provokers. Mental stimulators are useful to refocus the group on the topic at hand or to stimulate the brain and get participants back into a learning mood.

Make sure to use these types of activities purposefully and strategically. The audience should have a sense of why you are doing them. Using simple statements such as "Let's get our minds focused back on the learning process by starting with this simple quiz" or "Let's wake up our brains this afternoon by examining this trivia test" will help participants understand why you are doing the activity or exercise.

When used correctly, mental stimulators literally create energy in the group. You can see the physical energy increase through the mental stimulation. The activities included here are easy to use. Copy them and hand them out to participants — or read them to the group at appropriate times. Enjoy these mental stimulators!

SCORE! Two
More
Super
Closers
Openers
Reviews
Energizers
for
Enhanced
Training
Results

ENERGIZERS

ENERGIZERS

ARE YOU SMARTER THAN A FIFTH GRADER?

Circle the correct answer.

1. Who did not sign the U.S. Constitution?
    a. Ben Franklin   b. George Washington   c. Alexander Hamilton
    d. John Hancock

2. What is the capital of Nebraska?
    a. Boise   b. Lincoln   c. Little Rock   d. Omaha

3. Common table salt is a chemical compound of:
    a. Sodium & chlorine   b. Sodium & chromium   c. Magnesium & potassium
    d. Magnesium & sodium

4. The decimal equivalent of ¾ inch is:
    a. .66 inches   b. .75 inches   c. .825 inches   d. 3.4 inches

5. What's the world's longest river?
    a. Yangtze   b. Amazon   c. Nile   d. Mississippi

6. What's the correct answer to this math problem: ¾ + ½ = _____:
    a. 3/8   b. 4/8   c. 6/4   d. 5/4

7. Which is the softest rock?
    a. Carbon   b. Talc   c. Graphite   d. Quartz

8. Which sentence is incorrect?
    a. He gave two too many dollars to her.   b. Their mother is over there.
    c. The dog will wag it's tail.   d. It's just a matter of time until it's over.

9. What is not true about carbon dioxide (CO_2)?
    a. It is called dry ice in solid form.   b. It contributes to global warming.
    c. It's colorless, tasteless and odorless.   d. It is a noble gas.

10. What is the longest river in the United States?
    a. Missouri   b. Mississippi   c. Rio Grande   d. Ohio

SCORE! Two
More
Super
Closers
Openers
Reviews
Energizers
for
Enhanced
Training
Results

ENERGIZERS

ARE YOU SMARTER THAN A FIFTH GRADER? Answers

1. Who did not sign the U.S. Constitution?
   a. Ben Franklin   b. George Washington   c. Alexander Hamilton
   d. John Hancock

2. What is the capital of Nebraska?
   a. Boise   **b. Lincoln**   c. Little Rock   d. Omaha

3. Common table salt is a chemical compound of:
   a. Sodium & chlorine   b. Sodium & chromium   c. Magnesium & potassium
   d. Magnesium & sodium

4. The decimal equivalent of ¾ inch is:
   a. .66 inches   **b. .75 inches**   c. .825 inches   d. 3.4 inches

5. What's the world's longest river?
   a. Yangtze   b. Amazon   **c. Nile**   d. Mississippi

6. What's the correct answer to this math problem: ¾ + ½ = _____:
   a. 3/8   b. 4/8   c. 6/4   **d. 5/4**

7. Which is the softest rock?
   a. Carbon   **b. Talc**   c. Graphite   d. Quartz

8. Which sentence is incorrect?
   a. He gave two too many dollars to her.   b. Their mother is over there.
   c. The dog will wag it's tail.   d. It's just a matter of time until it's over.

9. What is not true about carbon dioxide (CO_2)?
   a. It is called dry ice in solid form.   b. It contributes to global warming.
   c. It's colorless, tasteless and odorless.   **d. It is a noble gas.**

10. What is the longest river in the United States?
    a. Missouri   b. Mississippi   c. Rio Grande   d. Ohio

SCORE! Two
More
Super
Closers
Openers
Reviews
Energizers
for
Enhanced
Training
Results

ENERGIZERS

BEST MUSICAL ARTISTS

Fill in the blanks with artists listed at the bottom of the page.

1. Artist with the most consecutive Top 10 hits   _____

2. Artist with the best-selling single of all time   _____

3. Oldest singer to have a Top 10 hit in Britain   _____

4. Female artist with the most platinum albums   _____

5. First British group to have a number 1 single in the U.S.   _____

6. Top musical movie of all time   _____

7. Best female group of all time   _____

8. Artist with first million-selling single in the U.S.   _____

9. Oldest singer with number 1 single in the U.S.   _____

10. Female singer with number 1 best album   _____

11. Best-selling original soundtrack album of all time   _____

12. Male artist with the most platinum albums   _____

13. Artist with the most country music awards won   _____

14. Longest-running musical on Broadway   _____

15. Artists with the most number 1 singles in the U.S.   _____

16. Oldest female singer with a number 1 single in the U.S.   _____

Best Musical Artists Hints

Vince Gill	Louis Armstrong
Barbra Streisand	Elton John
The Supremes	Whitney Houston
Cher	*Cats*
Grease	Perry Como
Garth Brooks	Frank Sinatra
Elvis Presley	Tornados
The Beatles	
The Bodyguard	

SCORE! Two
More
Super
Closers
Openers
Reviews
Energizers
for
Enhanced
Training
Results

ENERGIZERS

BEST MUSICAL ARTISTS Answers

Answers were accurate as of the publication date of this book.

1. Artist with the most consecutive Top 10 hits   **Elvis Presley**

2. Artist with the best-selling single of all time   **Elton John**

3. Oldest singer to have a Top 10 hit in Britain   **Frank Sinatra**

4. Female artist with the most platinum albums   **Barbra Streisand**

5. First British group with a number 1 single in the U.S.   **Tornados**

6. Top musical movie of all time   *Grease*

7. Best female group of all time   **Supremes**

8. Artist with first million-selling single in the U.S.   **Perry Como**

9. Oldest singer with number 1 single in the U.S.   **Louis Armstrong**

10. Female singer with number 1 best album   **Whitney Houston**

11. Best-selling original soundtrack album of all time   *The Bodyguard*

12. Male artist with the most platinum albums   **Garth Brooks**

13. Artist with the most country music awards won   **Vince Gill**

14. Longest running musical on Broadway   *Cats*

15. Artists with the most number 1 singles in the U.S.   **The Beatles**

16. Oldest female singer with number 1 single in the U.S.   **Cher**

SCORE! Two
More
Super
Closers
Openers
Reviews
Energizers
for
Enhanced
Training
Results

ENERGIZERS

FAMOUS DATES IN HISTORY

Fill in the blanks with dates listed at the bottom of the page.

1. First person to orbit earth – Yuri Gagarin   _____

2. Last eruption of Mt. Vesuvius – Italy   _____

3. First successful descent of Niagara Falls   _____

4. UFO lands in Roswell, New Mexico   _____

5. First patent issued in the U.S.   _____

6. Edmund Hillary climbs Mt. Everest   _____

7. First Bugs Bunny cartoon released   _____

8. Largest Chinook salmon caught (97 lbs.)   _____

9. Date the United States ratified the UN Charter   _____

10. Fidel Castro becomes president of Cuba   _____

11. Neil Armstrong walked on the moon   _____

12. First bottle of Coca-Cola sold in the U.S.   _____

13. First million-selling record in the U.S.   _____

14. Orville and Wilbur Wright's first flight   _____

15. First perfect game pitched in baseball   _____

16. M*A*S*H* farewell special aired   _____

17. First circumnavigation of the globe
    in less than 80 days   _____

Famous Dates in History Hints

June 12, 1880	October 24, 1901
March 14, 1958	May 17, 1985
April 12, 1961	November 2, 1976
December 16, 1631	January 25, 1890
July 31, 1790	February 28, 1983
July 8, 1947	December 17, 1903
May 29, 1953	August 8, 1945
July 16, 1969	May 1886
April 30, 1938	

SCORE! Two
More
Super
Closers
Openers
Reviews
Energizers
for
Enhanced
Training
Results

ENERGIZERS

FAMOUS DATES IN HISTORY Answers

1.	First person to orbit earth – Yuri Gagarin	**April 12, 1961**
2.	Last eruption of Mt. Vesuvius – Italy	**Dec. 16, 1631**
3.	First successful descent of Niagara Falls	**Oct. 24, 1901**
4.	UFO lands in Roswell, New Mexico	**July 8, 1947**
5.	First patent issued in the U.S.	**July 31, 1790**
6.	Edmund Hillary climbs Mt. Everest	**May 29, 1953**
7.	First Bugs Bunny cartoon released	**April 30, 1938**
8.	Largest Chinook salmon caught (97 lbs.)	**May 17, 1985**
9.	Date the United States ratified the UN Charter	**August 8, 1945**
10.	Fidel Castro becomes president of Cuba	**Nov. 2, 1976**
11.	Neil Armstrong walked on the moon	**July 16, 1969**
12.	First bottle of Coca-Cola sold in the U.S.	**May 1886**
13.	First million-selling record in the U.S.	**March 14, 1958**
14.	Orville and Wilbur Wright's first flight	**Dec. 17, 1903**
15.	First perfect game pitched in baseball	**June 12, 1880**
16.	M*A*S*H* farewell special aired	**Feb. 28, 1983**
17.	First circumnavigation of the globe in less than 80 days	**Jan. 25, 1890**

SCORE! Two
More
Super
Closers
Openers
Reviews
Energizers
for
Enhanced
Training
Results

ENERGIZERS

LITTLE-KNOWN TRIVIAL TIDBITS

Write your answers on the lines.

1. In what musical key do most American car horns beep? _____

2. Which of the five senses develops earliest in life? _____

3. What is a dactylogram? _____

4. What's the only mammal that can't fly, but it can fly? _____

5. Whose figure did Walt Disney studios use as a model for Tinker Bell? _____

6. What appears when the sun activates your melanocytes? _____

7. What are you if your I.Q. is below 25? _____

8. What must a Mensa member be? _____

9. About what percent of the population has an I.Q. greater than 100? _____

10. What two numbers on a telephone dial don't have letters? _____

11. Where does the phone ring if you dial 1-202-456-1414? _____

12. How old are the horses that run in the Kentucky Derby? _____

13. What's the oldest college in the United States? _____

14. What's the oldest trophy competed for by professional athletes in North America? _____

15. What does the C stand for in the formula $E=MC^2$? _____

16. What did a McDonald's hamburger cost in 1963? _____

SCORE! Two More Super Closers Openers Reviews Energizers for Enhanced Training Results

ENERGIZERS

LITTLE-KNOWN TRIVIAL TIDBITS Answers

1. In what musical key do most American car horns beep?   **The key of F**

2. Which of the five senses develops earliest in life?   **Smell**

3. What is a dactylogram?   **A fingerprint**

4. What's the only mammal that can't fly, but it can fly?   **Man**

5. Whose figure did Walt Disney studios use as a model for Tinker Bell?   **Marilyn Monroe**

6. What appears when the sun activates your melanocytes?   **Freckles**

7. What are you if your I.Q. is below 25?   **An idiot**

8. What must a Mensa member be?   **A genius**

9. About what percent of the population has an I.Q. greater than 100?   **25**

10. What two numbers on a telephone dial don't have letters?   **One and zero**

11. Where does the phone ring if you dial 1-202-456-1414?   **The White House**

12. How old are the horses that run in the Kentucky Derby?   **3 years old**

13. What's the oldest college in the United States?   **Harvard**

14. What's the oldest trophy competed for by professional athletes in North America?   **The Stanley Cup in hockey**

15. What does the C stand for in the formula $E=MC^2$?   **The speed of light**

16. What did a McDonald's hamburger cost in 1963?   **15 cents**

SCORE! Two More Super Closers Openers Reviews Energizers for Enhanced Training Results

ENERGIZERS

MAYBE STUPID IS CONTAGIOUS!

Here are some actual label instructions on consumer goods.

On a children's cough medicine: "Do not drive a car or operate machinery after taking this medication." (We could reduce construction accidents considerably if we could just get those five-year olds off the forklifts!)

On a sleep aid product: "Warning: May cause drowsiness." (And what was my reason for taking this product again?!)

On most Christmas lights: "For indoor or outdoor use only." (As opposed to what?)

On a Japanese food processor: "Not to be used for the other use." (Well, at least they got our curiosity aroused!)

On a Swedish chainsaw: "Do not attempt to stop chain with your hands or genitals." (Was there a lot of this going on?)

On a hair dryer: "Do not use while sleeping." (Shucks, and that's the only time I have to work on my hair.)

On a bag of chips: "You could be a winner! No purchase necessary. Details inside." (This must be the shoplifter's special.)

On a tiramisu dessert (printed on the bottom): "Do not turn upside down." (Well, duh, a bit late, huh!)

On a bread pudding: "Product will be hot after heating." (No kidding!)

On packaging for an iron: "Do not iron clothes on body." (But wouldn't this save me more time?)

On a jar of peanuts: "Warning: contains nuts." (Talk about a news flash!)

On a child's Superman costume: "Wearing of this garment does not enable you to fly." (I guess we do have to tell our kids some things!)

SCORE! Two
More
Super
Closers
Openers
Reviews
Energizers
for
Enhanced
Training
Results

ENERGIZERS

ENERGIZERS

MEMORY TEST FOR OLDER KIDS

Read the questions below, and see how many answers you can recall from an earlier time. Each blank line is to be filled in with one word.

1. After the Lone Ranger saved the day and rode off into the sunset, the grateful citizens would ask, "Who was that masked man?" Invariably someone would answer, "I don't know, but he left this behind." What did the Lone Ranger leave behind? _____ _____ _____

2. When the Beatles first came to the United States in early 1964, we all watched them on The _____ _____ Show.

3. "Get your kicks on _____ _____."

4. "The story you are about to see is true. The names have been changed to _____ _____ _____."

5. "In the jungle, the mighty jungle, the _____ _____ _____."

6. Besides the Twist, the Mashed Potato, and the Watusi, we "danced" under a stick that was lowered in a dance called _____ _____.

7. "N E S T L É S. Nestlés makes the very best _____."

8. Satchmo was America's "Ambassador of Goodwill." This popular jazz trumpet player's real name was _____ _____.

9. What object "takes a licking but keeps on ticking"? _____ _____

10. Red Skelton's hobo character was named _____ _____ _____. Red ended his television show by saying, "Good night, and _____ _____ _____."

11. Some Americans protested the Vietnam War by burning their _____ _____.

12. The cute little car with the engine in the back and the trunk in the front was called a VW. What two other names was it called? _____ and _____.

13. In 1971, singer Don McLean sang a song about "the day the music died." This was a tribute to _____ _____.

14. The first satellite was placed into orbit by the Russians. It was called _____.

15. A big fad of the 50s and 60s was a large ring placed around the waist and twirled. It was called a _____-_____.

SCORE! Two More Super Closers Openers Reviews Energizers for Enhanced Training Results

ENERGIZERS

MEMORY TEST FOR OLDER KIDS Answers

1. A silver bullet

2. Ed Sullivan

3. Route 66

4. protect the innocent

5. lion sleeps tonight

6. The Limbo

7. chocolate

8. Louis Armstrong

9. Timex watch

10. Freddy the Freeloader. "may God bless!"

11. draft cards (Bras were also burned)

12. beetle and bug

13. Buddy Holly

14. Sputnik

15. hula-hoop

SCORE! Two
More
Super
Closers
Openers
Reviews
Energizers
for
Enhanced
Training
Results

ENERGIZERS

72

NEW DICTIONARY WORDS

Cirle the correct words for these definitions recently added to Merriam-Webster's Collegiate Dictionary.

1. Which word means "extremely large"?
   a. Largesse   b. Ginormous   c. Bigulous   d. Tremendor

2. Name "a plastic strip fastened to wrists that can be used as a restraint."
   a. Plasticuff   b. Restrainasol   c. Strapstraint   d. Flex-cuff

3. Name "a disastrous situation created by a powerful concurrence of factors."
   a. A perfect storm   b. A moon shot   c. A tsunami episode   d. A circus mess

4. Name "a style of Southern rap featuring repetitive chants and rapid dance rhythms."
   a. Street   b. Gangster   c. Crunk   d. Ranger

5. What is the correct name for "a soap opera produced in/televised in Latin America"?
   a. A telenovela   b. A latinopera   c. A Latin soap   d. A jabon opera

6. Which word refers to "the motion picture industry in India"?
   a. Hollywood West   b. Punjab media   c. Bollywood   d. Taj Mahallywood

7. Which word means "benches, gazebos and other structures used in landscaping"?
   a. Furniture-scape   b. Hardscape   c. Yardscape   d. Park benching

8. Name "the shoot on a standard salad plant."
   a. Microgreen   b. Tuber   c. Budder   d. Taproot

9. What term describes "a snowboard race with jumps and turns"?
   a. Board slalom   b. X-boarding   c. Goofy bounce   d. Snow boardcross

10. What is the term for "a decisive defeat"?
    a. Flex show   b. Smackdown   c. Punic victory   d. Stomp-fox

SCORE! Two
More
Super
Closers
Openers
Reviews
Energizers
for
Enhanced
Training
Results

ENERGIZERS

NEW DICTIONARY WORDS Answers

1. Which word means "extremely large"?
   a. Largesse   **b. Ginormous**   c. Bigulous   d. Tremendor

2. Name "a plastic strip fastened to wrists that can be used as a restraint"?
   a. Plasticuff   b. Restrainasol   c. Strapstraint   **d. Flex-cuff**

3. Name "a disastrous situation created by a powerful concurrence of factors."
   a. A perfect storm   b. A moon shot   c. A tsunami episode   d. A circus mess

4. Name "a style of Southern rap featuring repetitive chants and rapid dance rhythms."
   a. Street   b. Gangster   **c. Crunk**   d. Ranger

5. What is the correct name for "a soap opera produced in/televised in Latin America"?
   a. A telenovela   b. A latinopera   c. A Latin soap   d. A jabon opera

6. Which word refers to "the motion picture industry in India"?
   a. Hollywood West   b. Punjab media   **c. Bollywood**   d. Taj Mahallywood

7. Which word means "benches, gazebos and other structures used in landscaping"?
   a. Furniture-scape   **b. Hardscape**   c. Yardscape   d. Park benching

8. Name "the shoot on a standard salad plant."
   a. Microgreen   b. Tuber   c. Budder   d. Taproot

9. What term describes "a snowboard race with jumps and turns"?
   a. Board slalom   b. X-boarding   c. Goofy bounce   **d. Snow boardcross**

10. What is the term for "a decisive defeat"?
    a. Flex show   **b. Smackdown**   c. Punic victory   d. Stomp-fox

SCORE! Two
More
Super
Closers
Openers
Reviews
Energizers
for
Enhanced
Training
Results

ENERGIZERS

PUBLISHING TRIVIA

Name the books that begin with these words (and the authors for extra points):

Opening Line   **Book** (and author)

1. "In the beginning God …"   _____

2. "This is George. He lived in Africa."   _____

3. "Two households, both alike in dignity, in
    fair Verona where we lay our scene."   _____

4. "Life is difficult."   _____

5. "Chug, chug, chug. Puff, puff, puff.
    Ding-dong, ding-dong."   _____

6. "For many days we had been tempest-
    tossed."   _____

7. "Good is the enemy of great."   _____

8. "All children, except one, grow up."   _____

9. "He was an old man who fished alone in
    a skiff in the Gulf Stream …"   _____

10. "It's not about you."   _____

11. "'Where's papa going with that axe?'
    said Fern to her mother."   _____

12. "It was the best of times, it was the
    worst of times."   _____

13. "In a hole in the ground there
    lived a hobbit."   _____

14. "Not so long ago a monster came
    to the town of Castle Rock, Maine."   _____

SCORE! Two
More
Super
Closers
Openers
Reviews
Energizers
for
Enhanced
Training
Results

ENERGIZERS

PUBLISHING TRIVIA Answers

1. "In the beginning God …"

   Holy Bible
   (God)

2. "This is George. He lived in Africa."

   Curious George
   (H.A. Rey)

3. "Two households, both alike in dignity, in fair Verona where we lay our scene."

   Romeo and Juliet
   (Wm. Shakespeare)

4. "Life is difficult."

   The Road Less Traveled
   (Scott Peck)

5. "Chug, chug, chug. Puff, puff, puff. Ding-dong, ding-dong."

   The Little Engine that Could
   (Watty Piper)

6. "For many days we had been tempest-tossed."

   The Swiss Family Robinson
   (Johann David Wyss)

7. "Good is the enemy of great."

   From Good to Great
   (Jim Collins)

8. "All children, except one, grow up."

   Peter Pan
   (J. M. Barrie)

9. "He was an old man who fished alone in a skiff in the Gulf Stream …"

   Old Man and the Sea
   (Ernest Hemingway)

10. "It's not about you."

    The Purpose-Driven Life
    (Rick Warren)

11. "'Where's papa going with that axe?' said Fern to her mother."

    Charlotte's Web
    (E.B. White)

12. "It was the best of times, it was the worst of times."

    A Tale of Two Cities
    (Charles Dickens)

13. "In a hole in the ground there lived a hobbit."

    The Hobbit
    (J. R. R. Tolkien)

14. "Not so long ago a monster came to the town of Castle Rock, Maine."

    Cujo
    (Stephen King)

ENERGIZERS

SPELLING QUIZ

Circle the word that is spelled correctly and matches the given definition.

1. An incorrect sequence of letters composing a word:
a. mispelling   b. misspelling   c. mispeling   d. missspelling

2. A commissioned officer in the Army, Air Force or Marines:
a. coronel   b. cernel   c. colnel   d. colonel

3. A breed of German dogs with long bodies and short legs:
a. dachsund   b. dachshund   c. dachsun   d. dachund

4. Confusion or discomposure of mind:
a. embarassment   b. embarrasement   c. embarrassment   d. embarrassement

5. Conforming to a thermometric scale on which water boils at 212 degrees:
a. Fahrenheit   b. Farenheit   c. Fairenheit   d. Fairhenheit

6. A device containing bits of colored material that reflect in a variety of patterns:
a. kaleidoscope   b. kalidescope   c. kaleidascope   d. kalediscope

7. Personal items, articles of equipment, or accessories:
a. paraphennalia   b. paraphernalia   c. paraphenailia   d. paraphanalia

8. A meeting at an appointed place and time:
a. rondevous   b. rendevous   c. rendezvous   d. rondezous

9. A device creating or utilizing emptiness of space:
a. vaccum   b. vaccuum   c. vacum   d. vacuum

10. A detective story or history story:
a. whodunit   b. whodunnet   c. whodunitt   d. whodoneit

SCORE! Two
More
Super
Closers
Openers
Reviews
Energizers
for
Enhanced
Training
Results

ENERGIZERS

SPELLING QUIZ Answers

1. An incorrect sequence of letters composing a word:
a. mispelling   **b. misspelling**   c. mispeling   d. missspelling

2. A commissioned officer in the Army, Air Force or Marines:
a. coronel   b. cernel   c. colnel   **d. colonel**

3. A breed of German dogs with long bodies and short legs:
a. dachsund   **b. dachshund**   c. dachsun   d. dachund

4. Confusion or discomposure of mind:
a. embarassment   b. embarrasement   **c. embarrassment**   d. embarrassement

5. Conforming to a thermometric scale on which water boils at 212 degrees:
a. Fahrenheit   b. Farenheit   c. Fairenheit   d. Fairhenheit

6. A device containing bits of colored material that reflect in a variety of patterns:
a. kaleidoscope   b. kalidescope   c. kaleidascope   d. kalediscope

7. Personal items, articles of equipment, or accessories:
a. paraphennalia   **b. paraphernalia**   c. paraphenailia   d. paraphanalia

8. A meeting at an appointed place and time:
a. rondevous   b. rendevous   **c. rendezvous**   d. rondezous

9. A device creating or utilizing emptiness of space:
a. vaccum   b. vaccuum   c. vacum   **d. vacuum**

10. A detective story or history story:
a. whodunit   b. whodunnet   c. whodunitt   d. whodoneit

SCORE! Two
More
Super
Closers
Openers
Reviews
Energizers
for
Enhanced
Training
Results

ENERGIZERS

STATE BIRDS

From the list below, choose each state's official bird, and write it on the line next to the corresponding state.

1. Arizona   _____

2. Arkansas   _____

3. Colorado   _____

4. Illinois   _____

5. Indiana   _____

6. Georgia   _____

7. Iowa   _____

8. Florida   _____

9. Maine   _____

10. Michigan   _____

11. Mississippi   _____

12. Nevada   _____

13. New Mexico   _____

14. North Carolina   _____

15. Ohio   _____

16. Oklahoma   _____

17. Pennsylvania   _____

18. South Dakota   _____

19. Tennessee and Texas   _____

20. Virginia and West Virginia   _____

21. Washington   _____

22. Wyoming   _____

State Birds Hints

Cactus Wren	Scissor-tailed Flycatcher	American Robin
Lark Bunting	Ring-tailed Pheasant	Brown Thrasher
Mountain Bluebird	Black-capped Chickadee	Ruffed Grouse
Roadrunner	Mockingbird (4)	Western Meadowlark
Eastern Goldfinch	Cardinal (5)	Willow Goldfinch

SCORE! Two More Super Closers Openers Reviews Energizers for Enhanced Training Results

ENERGIZERS

STATE BIRDS Answers

1.	Arizona	**Cactus Wren**
2.	Arkansas	**Mockingbird**
3.	Colorado	**Lark Bunting**
4.	Illinois	**Cardinal**
5.	Indiana	**Cardinal**
6.	Georgia	**Brown Thrasher**
7.	Iowa	**Eastern Goldfinch**
8.	Florida	**Mockingbird**
9.	Maine	**Black-capped Chickadee**
10.	Michigan	**American Robin**
11.	Mississippi	**Mockingbird**
12.	Nevada	**Mountain Bluebird**
13.	New Mexico	**Roadrunner**
14.	North Carolina	**Cardinal**
15.	Ohio	**Cardinal**
16.	Oklahoma	**Scissor-tailed Flycatcher**
17.	Pennsylvania	**Ruffed Grouse**
18.	South Dakota	**Ring-tailed Pheasant**
19.	Tennessee and Texas	**Mockingbird**
20.	Virginia and West Virginia	**Cardinal**
21.	Washington	**Willow Goldfinch**
22.	Wyoming	**Western Meadowlark**

SCORE! Two
More
Super
Closers
Openers
Reviews
Energizers
for
Enhanced
Training
Results

ENERGIZERS

USELESS THINGS TO KNOW

Write your answers on the lines.

1. What is the strongest muscle in the human body? _____

2. How many calories are used up by banging your head against a wall for one hour? _____

3. On average, how much longer do right-handed people live than left-handed people? _____

4. What animal kills more people than plane crashes each year? _____

5. What is the longest English word typed with only the left hand on a computer keyboard? _____

6. What famous author invented the words "bump" and "assassination"? _____

7. What is unique about the following sentence: "The quick brown fox jumps over the lazy dog"? _____

8. What is a unique fact about the names of all the continents? _____

9. Which country has more English speakers than the U.S.? _____

10. What is the smallest country in the world, with a size of just 108 acres, and a population of about 1,000? _____

11. What is the shortest complete sentence in the English language? _____

12. How many U.S. presidents were an only child? _____

SCORE! Two
More
Super
Closers
Openers
Reviews
Energizers
for
Enhanced
Training
Results

ENERGIZERS

USELESS THINGS TO KNOW Answers

1. What is the strongest muscle in the human body?   **The tongue**

2. How many calories are used up by banging your head against a wall for one hour?   **150 calories**

3. On average, how much longer do right-handed people live than left-handed people?   **Nine years**

4. What animal kills more people than plane crashes each year?   **The donkey**

5. What is the longest English word typed with only the left hand on a computer keyboard?   **Stewardesses**

6. What famous author invented the words "bump" and "assassination"?   **Shakespeare**

7. What is unique about the following sentence: "The quick brown fox jumps over the lazy dog"?   **It uses every letter in the alphabet.**

8. What is a unique fact about the names of all the continents?   **They all start and end with the same letter.**

9. Which country has more English speakers than the U.S.?   **China**

10. What is the smallest country in the world, with a size of just 108 acres and a population of about 1,000?   **Vatican City**

11. What is the shortest complete sentence in the English language?   **I am.**

12. How many U.S. presidents were an only child?   **None**

SCORE! Two
More
Super
Closers
Openers
Reviews
Energizers
for
Enhanced
Training
Results

ENERGIZERS

VOCABULARY QUIZ

Circle the word that matches the given definition.

1. Which word means "a condition of uncertainty"?
    a. quandary   b. quixotic   c. quarantined   d. quarrelsome

2. Which word means "proper behavior or conduct"?
    a. decorum   b. prosperity   c. conducive   d. ubiquitous

3. Which word means "the act of subtracting"?
    a. substantiate   b. deduction   c. lassitude   d. lessitude

4. Which word means "having a carefree, self-confident air"?
    a. omnipotent   b. flighty   c. jaunty   d. appropriated

5. Which term means "using few words"?
    a. laconic   b. tertiary   c. litigious   d. verbally jocund

6. Which term means "a figure of speech in which a comparison is made"?
    a. metamorphosis   b. metaphor   c. metalingual   d. metafiction

7. Which term means "a cloud of interstellar gas and dust"?
    a. abscond   b. corona   c. wormhole   d. nebula

8. Name a "poisonous, unstable form of oxygen that reflects ultraviolet rays."
    a. heavy water   b. neutron   c. ozone   d. socksogen

9. Which word refers to "a plant tissue that transports nutrients within plants"?
    a. stomota   b. pistil   c. phloem   d. chlorophyll

10. Which word means "to hesitate in a course of action"?
    a. cultivate   b. moratorium   c. vacillate   d. subjugate

SCORE! Two
More
Super
Closers
Openers
Reviews
Energizers
for
Enhanced
Training
Results

ENERGIZERS

VOCABULARY QUIZ Answers

1. Which word means "a condition of uncertainty"?
   a. quandary   b. quixotic   c. quarantined   d. quarrelsome

2. Which word means "proper behavior or conduct"?
   a. decorum   b. prosperity   c. conducive   d. ubiquitous

3. Which word means "the act of subtracting"?
   a. substantiate   **b. deduction**   c. lassitude   d. lessitude

4. Which word means "having a carefree, self-confident air"?
   a. omnipotent   b. flighty   **c. jaunty**   d. appropriated

5. Which term means "using few words"?
   a. laconic   b. tertiary   c. litigious   d. verbally jocund

6. Which term means "a figure of speech in which a comparison is made"?
   a. metamorphosis   **b. metaphor**   c. metalingual   d. metafiction

7. Which term means "a cloud of interstellar gas and dust"?
   a. abscond   b. corona   c. wormhole   **d. nebula**

8. Name a "poisonous, unstable form of oxygen that reflects ultraviolet rays."
   a. heavy water   b. neutron   **c. ozone**   d. socksogen

9. Which word refers to "a plant tissue that transports nutrients within plants"?
   a. stomota   b. pistil   **c. phloem**   d. chlorophyll

10. Which word means "to hesitate in a course of action"?
    a. cultivate   b. moratorium   **c. vacillate**   d. subjugate

SCORE! Two
More
Super
Closers
Openers
Reviews
Energizers
for
Enhanced
Training
Results

ENERGIZERS

WEATHER PHENOMENON

Fill in the blank in the right-hand column with the answer to the description on the left. Number one is completed as an example.

1. Partially melted snow or ice   *Slush*

2. Violent, rotating windstorm   _____

3. Severe, tropical cyclone   _____

4. Natural and perceptible movement of air
    parallel to/along the ground   _____

5. Covered or obscured with clouds or mist   _____

6. Solid precipitation in the form of white
    or translucent ice crystals   _____

7. A sudden rainstorm   _____

8. Transparent frozen or partially-frozen raindrops   _____

9. Water condensed from atmospheric vapor   _____

10. Mass of fine droplets of water near the earth   _____

11. Precipitation in the form of pellets of ice and hard snow   _____

12. Condensed water vapor in cloudlike masses   _____

13. Soft mud or slush   _____

14. Rotating column of air accompanied by funnel-shaped
    downward extension of cloud   _____

15. Visible body of very fine droplets of water   _____

SCORE! Two More Super Closers Openers Reviews Energizers for Enhanced Training Results

ENERGIZERS

WEATHER PHENOMENON Answers

1.	Partially melted snow or ice	**Slush**
2.	Violent, rotating windstorm	**Cyclone**
3.	Severe, tropical cyclone	**Hurricane**
4.	Natural and perceptible movement of air parallel to/along the ground	**Wind**
5.	Covered or obscured with clouds or mist	**Overcast**
6.	Solid precipitation in the form of white or translucent ice crystals	**Snow**
7.	A sudden rainstorm	**Cloudburst**
8.	Transparent frozen or partially-frozen raindrops	**Sleet**
9.	Water condensed from atmospheric vapor	**Rain**
10.	Mass of fine droplets of water near the earth	**Mist**
11.	Precipitation in the form of pellets of ice and hard snow	**Hail**
12.	Condensed water vapor in cloudlike masses	**Fog**
13.	Soft mud or slush	**Slop**
14.	Rotating column of air accompanied by funnel-shaped downward extension of cloud	**Tornado**
15.	Visible body of very fine droplets of water	**Cloud**

SCORE! Two
More
Super
Closers
Openers
Reviews
Energizers
for
Enhanced
Training
Results

ENERGIZERS

"WHO SAID" TRIVIAL TIDBITS

Name the person who made these famous statements.

1. "Honey, I forgot to duck." _____

2. "I only regret that I have but one life to give for my country." _____

3. "I have a dream today." _____

4. "Your partner is not a mind reader. You have to say, 'I need a little more of this, or I need a little less of that.'" _____

5. "When I look at my children, I say 'Lillian, you should have stayed a virgin.'" _____

6. "I float like a butterfly, sting like a bee." _____

7. "God bless us, everyone." _____

8. "There is nothing in the Bible that says I must wear rags." _____

9. "Where have you gone, Joe DiMaggio?" _____

10. "Feed 'em, love 'em, and leave 'em alone." _____

11. "I am not a crook." _____

12. "All you need to fly is lovely things and fairy dust." _____

13. "Candy is dandy, but liquor is quicker." _____

14. "But, soft. What light at yonder window breaks?" _____

15. "I never met a man I didn't like." _____

16. "It's not the men in my life, it's the life in my men." _____

17. "At a certain village in La Mancha, which I shall not name..." _____

18. "As long as I am mayor, there will be law and order in Chicago." _____

SCORE! Two
More
Super
Closers
Openers
Reviews
Energizers
for
Enhanced
Training
Results

ENERGIZERS

"WHO SAID" TRIVIAL TIDBITS Answers

1.	"Honey, I forgot to duck."	**President Ronald Reagan, after being shot**
2.	"I only regret that I have but one life to give for my country."	**Nathan Hale, being hanged**
3.	"I have a dream today."	**Martin Luther King Jr.**
4.	"Your partner is not a mind reader. You have to say, 'I need a little more of this, or I need a little less of that.'"	**Dr. Ruth Westheimer, sex therapist**
5.	"When I look at my children, I say 'Lillian, you should have stayed a virgin.'"	**President Carter's mother, Lillian**
6.	"I float like a butterfly, sting like a bee."	**Boxer Muhammad Ali**
7.	"God bless us, everyone."	**Tiny Tim, in *A Christmas Carol***
8.	"There is nothing in the Bible that says I must wear rags."	**Reverend Billy Graham**
9.	"Where have you gone, Joe DiMaggio?"	**Simon and Garfunkel, in the song "Mrs. Robinson"**
10.	"Feed 'em, love 'em, and leave 'em alone."	**Pediatrician Dr. Benjamin Spock**
11.	"I am not a crook."	**President Richard Nixon**
12.	"All you need to fly is lovely things and fairy dust."	**Peter Pan**
13.	"Candy is dandy, but liquor is quicker."	**Poet Ogden Nash**
14.	"But, soft. What light at yonder window breaks?"	**Romeo, in *Romeo and Juliet***
15.	"I never met a man I didn't like."	**Will Rogers, American statesman**
16.	"It's not the men in my life, it's the life in my men."	**Actress Mae West**
17.	"At a certain village in La Mancha, which I shall not name…"	**Don Quixote, in *Man of La Mancha***
18.	"As long as I am mayor, there will be law and order in Chicago."	**Chicago Mayor Richard J. Daley**

SCORE! Two
More
Super
Closers
Openers
Reviews
Energizers
for
Enhanced
Training
Results

ENERGIZERS

WORLD CAPITALS

Fill in the blanks below with the countries that correspond to the capital city.

1. Havana   _____
2. Copenhagen   _____
3. Brasilia   _____
4. Algiers   _____
5. Bangkok   _____
6. Tunis   _____
7. London   _____
8. Washington, D.C.   _____
9. Hanoi   _____
10. Paris   _____
11. Berlin   _____
12. Guatemala City   _____
13. Budapest   _____
14. Dublin   _____
15. Tokyo   _____
16. Seoul   _____
17. Warsaw   _____
18. Moscow   _____
19. City of San Marino   _____
20. Monaco   _____

World Capitals Hints

Brazil	France	Germany	Guatemala
Hungary	Ireland	Japan	Great Britain
South Korea	Poland	Russia	San Marino
Cuba	Denmark	Monaco	United States
Algeria	Tunisia	Vietnam	Thailand

SCORE! Two
More
Super
Closers
Openers
Reviews
Energizers
for
Enhanced
Training
Results

ENERGIZERS

WORLD CAPITALS Answers

Capital City	Country
1. Havana	**Cuba**
2. Copenhagen	**Denmark**
3. Brasilia	**Brazil**
4. Algiers	**Algeria**
5. Bangkok	**Thailand**
6. Tunis	**Tunisia**
7. London	**Great Britain**
8. Washington, D.C.	**United States**
9. Hanoi	**Vietnam**
10. Paris	**France**
11. Berlin	**Germany**
12. Guatemala City	**Guatemala**
13. Budapest	**Hungary**
14. Dublin	**Ireland**
15. Tokyo	**Japan**
16. Seoul	**South Korea**
17. Warsaw	**Poland**
18. Moscow	**Russia**
19. City of San Marino	**San Marino**
20. Monaco	**Monaco**

SCORE! Two
More
Super
Closers
Openers
Reviews
Energizers
for
Enhanced
Training
Results

ENERGIZERS

ENERGIZERS

Physical Activators provide a stretch — and often a learning point, too!

Great presentations and training sessions keep participants energized through the use of effective presentation methods as well as mental stimulators and physical activators. This section of *SCORE! Two* will offer a variety of energizers to **keep participants active and engaged.**

Energizers are useful throughout a session and probably are most useful during these times: after lunch, after a break, when the room temperature is too warm, and during the middle of a long content presentation.

This section of the book contains two types of energizers. Part two is the Physical Activators that get the body moving. These activities are often childlike, competitive and fun. They range from simple stretching exercises to those that involve fairly sophisticated brain-body coordination. Some of these physical activators are also designed to be controlled stretch breaks, thus creating a double win — a stretch for the participants while communicating a learning point.

Make sure to use these types of activities purposefully and strategically. The audience should have a sense of why you are doing them. Using simple statements such as "Okay, let's stand and get the body moving so we can continue learning" will help participants understand why you are doing the activity or exercise.

When used correctly, physical activators will get participants back into a learning mood with a refreshed body and a refocused mind. Although many of these are not content-related, most participants will make the connection between the activity and the purpose for which it was intended — to help the learning process. Enjoy these physical activators!

SCORE! Two
More
Super
Closers
Openers
Reviews
Energizers
for
Enhanced
Training
Results

ENERGIZERS

ENERGIZERS

AIR WRITING

Purpose: To create energy by getting participants up and moving

Audience: Any group size

Time: 2–3 minutes

Space: Enough space for participants to move freely without hitting each other

Materials: None

Budget: None

Application: Use this as an energizer any time during the day when fatigue is setting in.

Process:
1. Ask participants to stand. Tell them you are going to have them do some physical movement to "wake up your body — and your brain."

2. Instruct them to write their name in the air in cursive. You model it as you ask them to do it. Have them do it in this order:
   - With their dominant hand
   - With their nondominant hand
   - With their dominant elbow
   - With their nondominant elbow
   - With their hip (this one usually generates much laughter)

Cautions: Be aware of anyone with physical disabilities who may not be able to do this.

SCORE! Two
More
Super
Closers
Openers
Reviews
Energizers
for
Enhanced
Training
Results

ENERGIZERS

ALPHABET FREEZE

Purpose: Physical stretch break

Audience: Any size

Time: 5–10 minutes

Space: Enough room for people to move around

Materials: None

Budget: None

Application: Give participants a stretch break, a get-to-know-you exercise and/or a way to revisit content.

Process:

1. Have the group number off one, two, one, two. Have the number ones line up on one side of the room and the number twos line up on the other side of the room and face each other.

2. Ask participants to begin reciting the alphabet in unison. Let them continue for a while and then call out "STOP!" Ask them to identify the letter they stopped on. They must find a partner from the other side of the room and share something about themselves that begins with that letter. For example, if the letter is G, they might say, "I am gregarious, gorgeous, a go-getter," etc.

3. Repeat the exercise again, stopping at a different letter. Have them identify the letter and get a new partner. Using the new letter, have them share either something they have learned in the program or something they are looking forward to in the next few months. Repeat the process a few more times, altering the sharing activity.

Cautions: Avoid stopping on difficult letters such as "Q" or "X."

Variations: You may be very specific about what you would like them to share with one another depending on your objective for using this exercise.

SCORE! Two
More
Super
Closers
Openers
Reviews
Energizers
for
Enhanced
Training
Results

ENERGIZERS

GO FISH

Purpose:	To get people moving and to create new groups
Audience:	Any size
Time:	5–10 minutes
Space:	Enough room for people to move around
Materials:	A deck of Go Fish cards and four small prizes. The prizes may consist of a candy bar, bag of pretzels, highlighter, pen, note pad, etc.
Budget:	Cost of cards and prizes
Application:	Provide an activity that will energize participants
Process:	1. Tell participants it is time for a stretch break and that they will all be going fishing. Shuffle the deck of Go Fish cards and distribute two different fish cards per person. Ask them to stand and move to a different part of the room. Your purpose is to have them working with members of the group other than those they were sitting with.
	2. Begin by saying, "You've all been given a few fish cards. The object of this activity is to find three other people to complete one set of fish cards. All four fish in your set must be the same. You must have a total of four people to complete your set." Tell them that the first group of four to complete a set of fish will win a prize and will be asked to share some information with the group.
	3. After 5 minutes, if no one is able to complete a set of four fish, they may trade in their two cards for two new cards with you.
	4. Once you have a winning quartet, award the prizes and ask members of the winning team to sing a song, tell a joke or recite a poem. This usually generates a lot of laughter.
Cautions:	If this is a very large group, you may need two decks of cards. If your group is very small, just pull out a few of the sets of fish (each set of fish consists of four cards). People may trade cards if necessary to create the groups.
Variations:	This exercise may also be used as a review exercise by asking the winning team to share an insight from the training content.

SCORE! Two
More
Super
Closers
Openers
Reviews
Energizers
for
Enhanced
Training
Results

ENERGIZERS

MAKE A LINK

Purpose: This exercise is particularly useful in helping your participants get to know one another while engaging in a physical activity.

Audience: 6–10 people per group is ideal. With larger audiences, divide them into subgroups of 4–6 each.

Time: 10–12 minutes, up to 20 minutes if the exercise is serving your purpose

Space: A space large enough for groups to stand in a circle facing each other

Materials: A rope or heavy piece of string for each group — one foot of rope per person. Groups of 6–10 people would require a 10-foot rope.

Budget: Cost for rope or heavy string

Application: This activity provides participants the opportunity to build deeper relationships by "linking" life experiences with others, and possibly linking to class content, as well.

Process:
1. Begin by asking your participants to think of a story about themselves that they would be willing to share with the group. This could be a vacation they have taken, a project they've completed, or simply a life experience they've had. Tell the group they will be participating in an activity designed to learn more about one another. Give an example: share a story about yourself, keeping it to about 1 minute. Then organize participants in groups of six to 10 people who stand in a circle one foot apart and face each other.

2. Ask for one volunteer in each group to begin the process by sharing a story about themselves. Give a rope to the volunteer in each group and ask them to hold the rope exactly in the middle, so the rope will hang down on each side of them equally.

3. Tell them that the volunteer will begin telling her story. As soon as any member of the group can "make a link" with that person, he should identify himself as a "link," quickly stand next to the first person and take the rope. (The first person continues to hang onto the rope, as well.) Then the second person begins to tell the group something about himself and how it "links" to the first person. For example, the first person might begin by talking about a vacation to the San Diego Zoo and experiencing a camel ride. The next person might jump in as the first link and begin by

ENERGIZERS

MAKE A LINK

sharing his experience at another zoo or riding a camel in Saudi Arabia, or experiencing something else in San Diego. The links can go anywhere or have any connection that the participants choose.

4. The process continues until all members have made a link and everyone is holding a piece of rope.

5. End the activity by asking them to continue to find links with one another throughout the workshop.

Variations: You may want to make this activity directly relate to a theme or work activity by giving them a specific topic to talk about (i.e., customer service experiences, etc.).

SCORE! Two
More
Super
Closers
Openers
Reviews
Energizers
for
Enhanced
Training
Results

ENERGIZERS

PAINT THE ROOM

Purpose: Physical stretch break

Audience: Any size

Time: 2–4 minutes

Space: Enough room to stand and move the body without hitting others

Materials: None

Budget: None

Application: Provide an activity that will energize participants

Process:

1. Tell participants you have just received a memo that says the room must be painted by the end of the day. Inform them that they are going to start painting the room immediately. Tell them it would be best if they would just follow your directions.

2. Ask them to stand and pick up their paintbrush. (You model picking up an imaginary paintbrush and give these instructions):

   A. "Let's begin by painting the wall." (Using an up-and-down motion, begin painting an imaginary wall.)

   B. After 20 seconds say, "That looks good, let's start rolling the ceiling." (Again, pick up an imaginary roller and start making a rolling motion toward the ceiling.)

   C. After 20 seconds announce, "That looks great. It looks like this other wall will need some sanding before we can paint it, so let's use our elbows to sand the wall." (Using a circular motion, begin moving your elbow in circles.)

   D. After 20 seconds say, "You missed a few spots on the ceiling; perhaps we can reach them with our heads." (Begin jumping up and down and bobbing your head toward the ceiling.)

   E. After 20 seconds, let them know they have completed the painting job, but they now have to clean up some of the paint spills on the floor. Say, "Let's make this easy. Just drop a rag on the floor and clean it up with your foot." (Drop an imaginary rag on the floor and start swishing your right foot back and forth.) "Okay, now use the other foot." (Switch to your left foot.)

   Thank them for painting.

Cautions: Allow participants to opt out if they have physical limitations.

Variations: Use your creativity to "paint the room" in any way you choose!

SCORE! Two
More
Super
Closers
Openers
Reviews
Energizers
for
Enhanced
Training
Results

ENERGIZERS

PASS THE TOILET PAPER

Purpose: Physical stretch break

Audience: Any size

Time: 5–10 minutes

Space: Enough room for people to move around

Materials: A roll or two of toilet paper depending on the size of your group

Budget: Cost of toilet paper

Application: Give participants a stretch break and a get-to-know-you activity.

Process:

1. Pass around a roll of toilet paper to the group and tell them to take what they need. Give no further directions.

2. Once everyone has taken the amount of toilet paper they need, ask them to stand and find a partner who is not sitting at their table. Once they have a partner, tell them to share a fact about themselves for each square of toilet paper they took.

3. Once everyone has completed sharing, they return to their seats.

Variations: This can also be a revisit exercise by having participants share a learning point or action idea from the workshop for each square of toilet paper they took.

SCORE! Two
More
Super
Closers
Openers
Reviews
Energizers
for
Enhanced
Training
Results

ENERGIZERS

PERCEPTION PUZZLER

Purpose: Use this as a physical stretch break that makes a point

Audience: Any size

Time: 1–2 minutes

Space: Enough room for everyone to stand

Materials: None

Budget: None

Application: Provide an activity that will energize participants and make a point about a change in perception.

Process:

1. Ask participants to stand and point their index finger (either hand) at the ceiling. Tell them to rotate their finger in a clockwise direction, paying special attention to the direction.

2. Ask them to continue to rotate their finger, and slowly move their hand down to their eye level and then to their chest level, all the while continuing to rotate their finger.

3. Now ask them to notice the direction their finger is rotating. If they do this correctly, their finger will now be rotating in a counterclockwise direction.

4. Ask them to continue rotating their finger, and then raise it again to chest level, then eye level, and then above their head again. Their finger will now be rotating clockwise again.

Debrief: Ask participants to talk about perceptions. What is the power of perception? Do we ever see things one way while someone else sees them another way? What's the value of examining our perceptions?

SCORE! Two
More
Super
Closers
Openers
Reviews
Energizers
for
Enhanced
Training
Results

ENERGIZERS

100   © 2008 Creative Training Techniques Press www.bobpikegroup.com

SEMINAR TRIATHLON

Purpose: Give participants a physical stretch break

Audience: Any size

Time: 5 minutes

Space: Minimal space needed for participants to stand by their chairs

Materials: None

Budget: None

Application: Provide an exercise that creates energy and gives each participant a physical energizer.

Process:
1. Tell participants it is time for a stretch break. Ask participants if anyone has done a triathlon. If so, congratulate them. Now say, "Everyone will have the opportunity to participate in a seminar triathlon. You will each have a chance to jog, swim and bike right here in this seminar room. Are you ready?"

2. Ask participants to stand and leave space between each other so they don't bump or run into anyone. Explain they will begin with a 20-mile jog. Tell them they will just jog in place, and you'll be running with them. Say, "Okay, let's get going." Begin by jogging in place, and count out loud to 20. Stop jogging after 20 and say, "Great job, give yourselves a hand." Everyone applauds.

3. "Now we are going to swim 20 laps. Ready, let's begin." Stand in place and begin moving your arms as though you are doing the crawl, and count to 20. After 20 say, "Nice job, you are all great swimmers."

4. "For the last segment of the triathlon we'll be biking 20 miles. Everyone, sit in a chair, and scoot a little forward in the chair and lean back. Ready bikers? Let's go." Lift your legs slightly and begin cycling in the air, and count to 20. After 20 say, "Fantastic, you have all completed the seminar triathlon. Give someone a high-five and return to your seats."

Cautions: Allow participants that are physically disabled or unable to do physical exercises to opt out of this activity.

Variations: Depending on the agility of the group, you can increase or decrease the number of seminar miles and laps you do.

SCORE! Two
More
Super
Closers
Openers
Reviews
Energizers
for
Enhanced
Training
Results

ENERGIZERS

STAND WHEN FINISHED

Purpose: This is a useful stretching exercise whenever you are having participants work individually on an activity.

Audience: Any size

Time: 1–2 minutes

Space: Enough room to stand and stretch

Materials: None

Budget: None

Application: Provide an activity that will energize participants and also let the instructor know when participants are done with an exercise.

Process:

1. Whenever you are going to assign participants an individual activity such as completing a computer exercise, or completing a worksheet, let them know in advance that when they finish the exercise, they should "please stand quietly and stretch for a few moments."

2. As participants begin to stand, you can get a sense of how many have completed the exercise. You may then judge when you call time for a completion of the exercise.

3. This activity provides three benefits by:
   - Giving participants a controlled stretch break
   - Helping you sense how close to completion they are
   - Creating a sense of urgency in those who are slow to finish

Cautions: Be careful not to overuse this activity as you don't want those who need more time to feel like there is something wrong with them.

SCORE! Two
More
Super
Closers
Openers
Reviews
Energizers
for
Enhanced
Training
Results

ENERGIZERS

STRETCH OUT

Purpose: To make the point that sometimes we have to move ourselves outside of our comfort zone to get better results

Audience: Any size audience

Time: 1–2 minutes

Space: Enough space for all participants to stretch out their arms without striking anyone else in the room

Materials: None

Budget: None

Application: Use this as an energizer during the day, especially when you want to make the point that sometimes we have to "stretch" outside of our comfort zone.

Process:

1. Ask everyone to stand, and tell them they are going to stretch outside of their comfort zone. Tell them to stretch their arms out straight on either side of their body (model this as you walk them through it). Have them point their left index finger straight out.

2. Now tell the participants to plant their feet on the ground and rotate their body to the left, holding their arm straight with their finger still pointing out. They should comfortably stretch as far as they can go. Tell them, "Now, mark a point in the room where your finger is pointing, and remember that point." Then have them rotate back to their starting position and drop their arms.

3. Tell participants that in a way, this point in the room represents their comfort zone — the place to which they naturally go, but usually don't go beyond. Ask them if they believe that most of the time it is possible to "stretch" outside of our regular comfort zone. Tell them that you are going to repeat the exercise, but before doing so, ask them to do some stretching exercises (whatever they are comfortable doing for just 30 seconds — or you may lead them in some short stretching exercises).

4. Now repeat step two above, encouraging your participants to "go farther" with their index finger this time. Tell them to "really stretch yourself, and see how far you can go beyond the original point where you pointed your finger — without straining any muscles." (Most participants can usually go several feet or more beyond their original point.)

SCORE! Two
More
Super
Closers
Openers
Reviews
Energizers
for
Enhanced
Training
Results

ENERGIZERS

STRETCH OUT

Debrief: Have participants share (either in small groups or as a whole group) their experience with the exercise. How much farther were they able to "stretch" themselves the second time? Why? How does this apply to their lives or to the topic of the day?

Cautions: Be alert to any physical limitations in the group. You may wish to allow anyone to "opt out" of the exercise if she so chooses.

Variations: Use this as an opener for a session when you're going to ask participants to do something that they don't think they can do, or that will stretch them.

SCORE! Two
More
Super
Closers
Openers
Reviews
Energizers
for
Enhanced
Training
Results

ENERGIZERS

104

THE LINEUP

Purpose: To get participants moving about and forming new groups

Audience: Minimum of 12

Time: 10–15 minutes

Space: Enough space to form a single-file line with all participants

Materials: None

Budget: None

Application: Use this as an energizer during the day; it also serves as a review technique.

Process:

1. Ask everyone in the class to form one line based on the date on which their birthday falls. Tell them they will not be able to talk or give any voice commands during the exercise. Give them 1 minute. Once the line is formed, divide the students into teams of equal size (about four to six per small group) by any method you choose (first four, second four, count-off, etc.).

2. Once the groups are formed, ask each group to list two or three ideas they've learned from today's session and how they see those ideas being implemented back at work.

3. Give them 4 minutes and then have the groups report out.

Variations: Use as an opening exercise. In a communications seminar, you could use this as a way to break participants into small groups, and then ask them what they learned from the nonverbal approach to forming their single-file line. Ask them how this might apply to the topic of today's session.

SCORE! Two
More
Super
Closers
Openers
Reviews
Energizers
for
Enhanced
Training
Results

ENERGIZERS

TIC-TAC-DOUGH

Purpose: To provide an energy break while creating an opportunity for participants to learn more about one another. This builds synergy among the class and also creates some healthy competition.

Audience: Works best with a group of 12–20

Time: 2 minutes to set up, and 6 minutes per round

Space: Room for participants at flip charts

Materials: Flip chart paper, tape, markers, pads of sticky notes, play money, and prizes

Budget: Cost of flip chart paper, markers, play money and three prizes. Prizes can be candy, pens/pencils/highlighters, coffee mugs, or any inexpensive prize.

Application: Create a physical stretch break, and have participants learn more about one another.

Process:

1. Prior to your training session, create "game questions" that reveal something about the participants (safe, comfortable information for you to share about the participants.) For example, you might know that one of the participants plays a clarinet, owns a poodle or drives a red Mustang. Simply turn the information into a question, such as "Who plays a clarinet?" or "Who owns a poodle?" or "Who drives a red Mustang?" Have participants create the game questions by writing something about themselves on a 3x5-inch card and giving this to you with their name on it before the class begins. Be sure to include yourself in the questions. The object of this activity is to guess the right answer and win some dough.

2. Here is how you play the game: When you see that participants might need a little energy break, tell them, "It is time to play Tic-Tac-Dough."

3. Inform the group they are going to play a version of tic-tac-toe called "Tic-Tac-Dough." Tell them they will have the opportunity to answer questions that reveal information about the participants in the room.

4. Have participants number around the room one, two, one, two, etc. Number ones are Os, the twos are Xs. Have the Os stand.

SCORE! Two
More
Super
Closers
Openers
Reviews
Energizers
for
Enhanced
Training
Results

ENERGIZERS

TIC-TAC-DOUGH

They must find an "X" partner who is sitting. Once everyone has a partner, have them come to the front of the room; each pair should take two different color markers, two sticky note pads and one piece of flip chart paper.

Each team finds a space on the wall to attach their chart paper. If possible, the charts should be a minimum of six feet apart. Ask them to divide their paper into quarters and draw a Tic-Tac-Toe game in each quarter of their paper.

See example below. Draw an example on your flip chart pad.

Let them know they will be playing four rounds of Tic-Tac-Dough throughout the day.

5. Tell them you will be reading questions aloud that reveal something about the participants. When you read the question aloud, they write their answer on the sticky note with their marker. Once written, they cannot change their answer. The first team member who gets the answer correct will get to place his X or O on one of the spaces on the Tic-Tac-Dough board.

6. Read the question. Wait 5 seconds and say, "Write your answer." Say the answer aloud. Whoever has the right answer gets to mark their X or O symbol on the chart. If both teammates get the answer right, they both get to place their X and O on the board. (Take turns going first if both get the right answer). If neither one answers correctly, neither places their X or O on the chart.

7. Each time a participant answers correctly, she gets $1 of play money. She runs up to you, as the banker, gets her money and goes back to her chart. (Have the money laid out on the table in the middle of the room or close to the teams so this process can go quickly). This creates physical activity and energy in the room. When one member of the team gets Tic-Tac-Dough (three Xs or Os in a line vertically, horizontally, or diagonally), they win $5.

8. The first round is over when one person wins Tic-Tac-Dough. Participants return to their seats. The charts stay on the wall for the next round.

ENERGIZERS

TIC-TAC-DOUGH

9. After playing four rounds, award Gold, Silver, and Bronze prizes to those persons with the highest, second highest and third highest amounts of money.

Cautions: Be sensitive to physical disabilities. If you have anyone in the room who cannot stand, play the game with teammates sitting at a table. However, participants ultimately achieve the purpose of this activity by standing.

Variations:

1. To save time, have teammates keep track of their wins with sticky dots on their chart (small dot for $1 and large dot for $5 and different color dots for each teammate). They collect their money at the end of the round. If you don't have dots, simply have them make hash marks on the chart.

2. This can also be a review exercise by writing test questions about the content you are teaching.

SCORE! Two
More
Super
Closers
Openers
Reviews
Energizers
for
Enhanced
Training
Results

ENERGIZERS

YOUR NAME IN LIGHTS!

Your name can SHOW UP IN LIGHTS as a contributor of an opener, a closer, a review technique or an energizer in our next publication.

Design and create any sort of opening and closing exercises.
Find new ways to energize your participants or create ways
to review or summarize content. We'd like to hear yours.
**If we publish your idea in our next *SCORE!* book,
you'll receive an updated copy with "YOUR NAME IN LIGHTS!"**

Copy this page and use the copy for your submission.
Describe/draw your idea briefly but completely.
Use the lines below and another sheet, if necessary,
or send us your submission by e-mail to Rich@MeissEducation.com.

We'll give you full credit for any ideas published. Thank you.

_____

_____

_____

_____

_____

YOUR NAME: _____

COMPANY (IF APPLICABLE): _____

ADDRESS: _____

PHONE: _____ FAX: _____

E-MAIL: _____

Submit ideas to
Rich@MeissEducation.com
or
Creative Training Techniques Press
14530 Martin Drive
Eden Prairie, MN 55344
Fax: 952-829-0260
www.BobPikeGroup.com

SCORE! Two
More
Super
Closers
Openers
Reviews
Energizers
for
Enhanced
Training
Results

SCORE! Two
More
Super
Closers
Openers
Reviews
Energizers
for
Enhanced
Training
Results

ABOUT THE AUTHORS

Rich Meiss has played a key role in the human resource industry since 1972, holding executive positions with Personal Dynamics, Inc., Carlson Learning Company and The Bob Pike Group. He is currently president of Meiss Education Institute.

Rich has personally trained over 50,000 trainers and leaders by conducting workshops and seminars and delivering keynote speeches in over 150 cities on four continents.

An inspiring speaker and interactive trainer, Rich's topics vary, but his theme always centers on increasing personal and organizational productivity through developing the human side of enterprise. Rich is an active member of the National Speakers Association and the American Society for Training and Development and has addressed his peers at national conferences.

Rich has co-authored training programs with Bob Pike, Dr. Denis Waitley, Dr. Michael O'Connor, William Mills and Dave Arch, and has published numerous articles in trade journals. He is author of the books, *GIFTS: Ideas to Enhance Your Work & Life* and *Warming Up the Crowd*. Special recognition includes being listed in *Who's Who in the Midwest* and *Emerging Leaders in America*.

Meiss Education Institute, located in Minneapolis, Minnesota, is a full-service training and consulting organization that offers seminars, speaking and coaching services, trainer/facilitator training and products that help organizations capitalize on their human resources. Contact Rich at 952-446-1586 or Rich@MeissEducation.com.

Bob Pike has developed and implemented training programs since 1969. Beginning as a representative for Master Education Industries, he received nine promotions in three and a half years, to senior vice president. During his five years as vice president of Personal Dynamics, Inc., that company grew from fewer than 4,000 enrollments per year to more than 80,000.

As founder and chairman of The Bob Pike Group and Creative Training Techniques Press, Bob leads sessions over 150 days per year covering topics like leadership, motivation, problem-solving, conflict management, team building and managerial productivity. More than 100,000 trainers have attended the Creative Training Techniques™ workshop. As a consultant, Bob has worked with such organizations as Pfizer, Upjohn, Hallmark Cards Incorporated and IBM. A member of the American Society for Training and Development since 1972, Bob has been active in many capacities and received ASTD's Council of Peers Award of Excellence.

An outstanding speaker, Bob was granted the professional designation of Certified Speaking Professional by the National Speakers Association. In 2007, he was voted one of the 20 most influential training professionals by Training Industry and received ISA's prestigious Thought Leader Award. He is editor of the *Creative Training Techniques Newsletter* and author of more than 10 videos and 20 training books including *The Creative Training Techniques Handbook* and co-author of *One-on-One Training, Dealing with Difficult Participants, 50 Creative Training Openers*, and *50 Creative Training Closers*. Bob can be reached by e-mail at BPike@BobPikeGroup.com or 800-383-9210 or 952-829-1954.

SCORE! Two
More
Super
Closers
Openers
Reviews
Energizers
for
Enhanced
Training
Results